Tea For Jean

One Family's Experience of the Adult Social Care System

Sue Cronk and Kim Kimber

This is a faithful account of events, backed up by our notes, diary entries and the Final Decision of the Local Government and Social Care Ombudsman.

Some names and identifying details have been changed to protect the privacy of individuals.

Cover design by Hutchins Creative Limited
www.hutchinscreative.co.uk

ISBN: 978-1-3999-6184-4

Contents

Introduction

It was a family joke that our mum would live to be 100. She was a strong, determined, independent woman, loved by all. That she would become a centenarian certainly seemed possible as the years ticked by. Having survived the Second World War and overcome personal tragedy as a young woman, in later life she faced widowhood and the disabling effects of chronic arthritis, osteoporosis and Alzheimer's disease with her usual positivity.

She lived to be ninety-six, a good age, but during the last six years of her life she suffered unnecessarily at the hands of some of those we trusted to care for her and was then cruelly shut away from her loved ones during a global pandemic. Had she received better care early on, from carers at home and in her first care home, and not been cut off from her family for the best part of a year, she may well have lived to receive her congratulatory 100th birthday card from King Charles to whose mother (Queen Elizabeth II) she bore a resemblance. We will never know. In truth, Alzheimer's is a cruel disease, and it was always going to catch up with her in the end, but we are saddened that those precious, final years with Mum were tainted by failures in the UK adult social care system and an out-of-touch government.

Privatisation of adult social care in the UK has meant the quality of care provided is not always equal. There are some excellent care providers who work tirelessly for the good of those they look after but, conversely, there are some who fail in their duty of care and fall short of the expected standards. We met examples of both during the time Mum needed some form of care and the difference is stark. What is shocking is that in 2023, the care system still appears to be a lottery. In many care homes, residents are comfortable and well-looked after, enjoying some kind of mental stimulation and physical activity each day. However, in others, they can spend long hours alone, unloved and uncared for, even during their final hours. Things have got to change.

The adult social care system needs government funding and reform. Life expectancy has steadily increased but living to a good age, sadly, does not always equate to being sound in mind and body, and increasing numbers of people need help in later years. The National Health Service and Community Care Act 1990 brought in changes in the way local social care functions were administered and responsibility for funding, planning and means testing community care services was transferred to local authorities. This meant they were now responsible for arranging funding for residential care and domiciliary care services such as home assistance. Inevitably, this has led to care being contracted out and ultimately privatised leading to greater disparity between care providers. Care homes were the responsibility of local councils until 2009 when the Care Quality Commission (CQC) was introduced to oversee them more closely.

In the early days of the new system, those in need of care in later life were able to receive support at home for longer, but back then there were far fewer people in the system. Care workers were less rushed and more able to assist each client with their specific needs and were not so affected by budget cuts and increased time pressures. The current system is overstretched and underfunded. At the time of writing, much has been promised by successive governments who continually renege on their promises, and the system is failing.

Our lovely mum, Jean, was diagnosed with Alzheimer's disease in 2015. At that time, we knew very little about the illness or what it would mean for Mum and our family. We couldn't have known it then but that was the start of a six-year journey, navigating our way through the UK adult social care system supporting Mum as best we could to ensure she was always well-looked after. We had little prior knowledge of the care system and few expectations other than Mum's welfare and well-being would always be at the forefront of every decision. Unfortunately, we were wrong. That day, back in 2015, signified the beginning of a turbulent, sometimes terrifying and incredibly sad time, when we would need to stand together and fight for our mum every step of the way. Our experiences, spanning six years, fall roughly into three two-year periods; care at home, Care Home 1 and Care Home 2.

A great deal has been written on the subject of Alzheimer's disease and what it is like living with or caring for someone with dementia, so that is not the focus of this book. We want to share our experience of the adult social care system, good and bad, in the hope it might help others in a similar situation, and aid them in making informed decisions for their loved ones. For it is only in having these difficult conversations and sharing our stories that real change can be brought about.

We have interspersed the chapters about caring for our mum after her diagnosis with Alzheimer's disease with shorter chapters about her life, to provide a snapshot of the amazing woman she was. Someone with hopes and dreams and a family who loved her dearly. Every person in care has a story to tell and their life should not be defined by the end, but rather celebrated for the unique individual they are.

This book is for those about to navigate the care system, who are facing care, or living in care, and especially all those who do not have a voice, or anyone to speak up for them. This book is for you, in loving memory of a very special lady, Jean Nancy, who to us was simply 'Mum'.

Sue & Kim x

Chapter 1
Care at Home

Mum was a widow who had lived alone since the death of our father in 2005. Dad died in hospital after a short illness and our experience, back then, had not been a good one (more of that later). As her daughters, and now next of kin, we vowed that Mum would receive better treatment when the time came for her to need extra care and support.

Mum was eighty when Dad passed away, already a good age, and in reasonably good health. In spite of the fact she suffered from osteoporosis and severe osteoarthritis, she rarely complained and didn't let it get her down or prevent her from doing things. It was an ongoing joke that if you left any items of clothing lying around, Mum would have the ironing board out, whether the garments needed pressing or not. We eventually resorted to hiding the ironing pile but still Mum would manage to find things to iron; anything from tea towels to socks, nothing escaped her.

She was independent and coped well on her own, looking after herself and keeping the house clean. She came from a generation where a newly swept front step was as important as a clean kitchen. If the net curtains needed washing, Mum would balance precariously on the back of the settee to take them down. If the lawn needed mowing or the garden weeding, she would be out with her sleeves rolled up. In fact, flowers were one of the things that always brought her joy. And she was resourceful, too, finding ingenious ways to manage difficult tasks, usually without so much as a nod to health and safety. Scissors and sharp knives were deployed to open anything from tins to letters and dining chairs and tables would be used to stand on to reach those hard to get to places.

For a long time, Mum used to cross the hazardous, busy main road near her home to the local newsagent to buy a daily paper. If grandchildren were visiting, she would often go back again to buy comics, sweets and treats. It worried us a great deal and we begged her to wait until we got there so that we could go to the shop for her, but our mum wasn't a waiting kind of woman. (In years gone by, if she decided a room needed decorating, Dad would come home to find her up a ladder stripping off the wallpaper.)

'I can manage,' she would say whenever we volunteered our help. 'Ooh, don't fuss.' In this time-pressured world, the family all had commitments and, being impatient, Mum didn't want to wait a day or so until someone could go round when, in her eyes, she was capable of doing it herself. For the most part, she succeeded.

The change in Mum's behaviour wasn't sudden or obvious. She could just be a bit forgetful sometimes or more short tempered than usual. She was often cross with herself because she couldn't remember things. Then she started to repeat herself and become anxious about trivial things, particularly if it involved a change in routine. Most of these symptoms we put down to old age but as Mum started to struggle with everyday tasks, we wondered if there could be a more sinister reason.

Looking to the future, we cautiously opened the conversation about sheltered housing, but Mum was having none of that. She wanted to continue to live in the house she had, by then, called home for over sixty years. Assuring us that she could manage, she refused to even discuss the possibility of a move, so we began to put things in place to make it easier for her to stay in her own home for as long as possible.

One of the first items to arrive was a walking frame, which Mum came to rely on more and more over the following years. Mum took her Zimmer frame everywhere, referring to it as her 'friend'. And indeed it was, helping her to retain her independence for some considerable time.

Next we bought her a comfortable, electric reclining armchair. It was easy to operate and literally lifted Mum onto her feet. It also tipped backwards and had a raised footrest when she wanted to put her feet up. The chair was a great success and made it much easier for her to get up, although there were one or two tense moments when it malfunctioned and she lost her famously wicked sense of humour.

We also sourced equipment such as a commode, so

that Mum didn't have to negotiate the trip to the bathroom in the middle of the night. She had a weak bladder, a legacy from her childbearing years, and needed to visit the toilet frequently. We raised the height of the downstairs toilet and installed a frame over the top so that Mum could use it to balance and to pull herself up. We also employed someone to help with domestic chores, but Mum was never completely satisfied with the cleaner's efforts and would redo everything the moment she left.

Every Thursday, Sue would take Mum to do the weekly food shop. Our mum valued punctuality and each week she would be sitting with her coat on, ahead of time, waiting. 'Where *have* you been, Susan?' she would ask. (It was always Susan, rather than Sue, when she was cross.)

At the supermarket, Mum would whiz around the shelves with surprising speed and agility and, again, be sat on one of the chairs beyond the tills, shopping packed in bags and paid for, waiting for her daughter. More than once, Sue was chided for her tardiness.

Mum loved to treat her grandchildren and, on one occasion, while shopping, picked up a coat for one of her granddaughters, who was then a young child. To her dismay, when she got home she realised she had forgotten to pay for it. Undeterred, out came her walking frame and she walked the one-mile distance, across very busy roads, and up and down a steep railway bridge, to rectify her mistake. When she arrived home, some considerable time later, she joyfully telephoned Sue and told her what had transpired, adding: 'It was lucky I went back; the coat was on sale and I wouldn't have got a discount otherwise.' Values of honesty and integrity had been instilled in her from a young age.

Later, when it became more difficult for Mum to get out, we took over food shopping completely, but would get told off if anything was substituted or unavailable. In reality, Mum was very grateful, and would reward anyone who helped her with tea and a warm smile (she made lunch for the central heating engineers every day when they were installing her new heating system). In fact, Mum always thought of others before herself. She was kind-hearted and selfless and would happily go without if someone else was in need. Through the years, many would feel the warmth of her welcome.

Initially, she continued to make her own meals, cooking a full roast dinner on a Sunday on the rare occasion she wasn't coming round to one of us. Later, we bought ready meals that could be stored in the freezer for her to defrost and heat up in the oven when required. (Mum always hated the microwave and largely refused to use it.) We would make up portions of Bolognese, cottage pie or casseroles and leave those in the freezer. We would also go round and make lunch. Later, when we had carers in, they were supposed to help with meals, but Mum didn't like to wait so would often be found in the kitchen, balancing precariously on her Zimmer frame with one hand, waving a bread knife around with the other. At one time, we tried a local 'meals on wheels' type service but this didn't work very well as Mum didn't really like the meals on offer and often the time of day they delivered didn't suit her routine.

She also liked to have several cups of tea throughout the day, which she would drink scalding hot, and it concerned us that she would use the kettle and then walk, mug in hand, back to her chair, while pushing her frame. We tried attaching a purpose-built tray to her walking frame, but she never quite got the hang of it and it only served to make the whole exercise even more dangerous.

Mum lived in an old house, with steep stairs, and it worried us to think of her negotiating them every night. We eventually persuaded her to let us put a bed in the downstairs front room. Up until this point, Mum had slept in the bed she had previously shared with Dad. The solid-framed double bed had been a fixture from as far back as we could remember and had been the cause of quite a few stubbed toes. There was no way this heavy bed could be moved easily and it would have taken up too much space downstairs. So we bought a spacious single bed with a safety rail that Mum could also use to help her get up. She had a mountain of pillows to prop her up and a new duvet. We added a wardrobe and the front lounge turned into a bedroom.

She was warm and comfortable, but most importantly, safe. Or so we believed! However, Mum would often let slip that the upstairs bedrooms needed a dust or hoover, then admit she had been up there to 'check on things'. We lived in fear of her falling down the stairs, especially as she had brittle bones.

Aside from her physical needs, Mum continued to be forgetful and, as time passed, could get quite confused by simple tasks. Each time she took the mental cognitive test to assess her memory and recall, arranged by our local hospital, she fared a little worse and, in 2015, our suspicions were confirmed. Mum was diagnosed with Alzheimer's disease. Back then, we knew very little about the illness or what to expect, but that was to change rapidly.

From the outset, we learnt as much as we could about Mum's condition. We read leaflets given to us by health care professionals and searched online for up-to-date information. The long-term outlook seemed bleak and, in the early days of Mum's diagnosis, we hoped old age would take her before she succumbed to this cruel disease. We had heard of people suffering from dementia not being able to remember their loved ones. This seemed to be particularly unkind; being robbed of something so precious, and the one thing you think no one can ever take away from you. We dreaded the day coming when Mum no longer recognised her daughters and close family.

Around this time, we attended a local four-week course run by the Alzheimer's Society. The information provided was extremely useful and we met other people in a similar situation and heard their stories. We were shocked by the way some people had to care for their loved ones day in, day out, with little outside help or respite. We wondered why more help wasn't available but, of course, it more often than not comes down to money.

The course leader made an analogy that was to be immensely helpful later on in understanding how to relate to Mum. She told us to imagine a tall bookcase where every shelf represents a year of a person's life, starting at the bottom from the day they were born. If the bookcase becomes unsteady, the 'books' or, in this case, memories, begin to tumble, falling from the top down. So short-term memories are lost first, while the early years tend to stay in place for much longer, the base having a stronger foundation. Thus, people suffering from dementia can often remember things that happened years ago but can't recall anything that happened yesterday. As the disease progressed, we found it was better to inhabit whatever year Mum found herself to be in, rather than add to her confusion and distress by correcting her. This could be tricky when she sometimes talked about loved ones who had passed, particularly our dad.

On one occasion Mum said she was tired after her long drive, having driven to the airport to pick up Dad. She was most insistent but her story was strange in more than one way. Our Dad had passed away several years previously, and in later life he rarely left the house. Even more odd was the fact that Mum had never learnt to drive, a fact she seemed to have overlooked (Dad had tried to teach her at one time, but she was too nervous and didn't persevere. According to family legend, a young Sue had jumped out of the car when Mum was behind the wheel!). But, on that day, Mum was convinced she could drive.

Early on in her diagnosis, Mum would have far more good days than bad. She would be her usual cheery self for a while and then become very forgetful and fretful, forgetting even the simplest things, but being aware she couldn't remember which she would find distressing. She needed lots of reassurance. We would tell her we forgot things all the time and not to worry as it was part of being human. Whenever possible, we tried not to focus on her forgetfulness and drew her attention to another subject.

One thing we found useful was a Memory Calendar, sold by the Alzheimer's Society. The upright, flip over, page a day calendar has the day, month and date clearly printed at the top of the page with plenty of space to write underneath. We would record birthdays, outings, visits and special dates well in advance, including what time to expect us. Mum then knew what was happening that day and could check if she forgot. If there was a day that we were unable to visit, we would leave little messages: 'We love you', 'See you tomorrow' or 'Sending love and hugs'.

However, there reaches a point in the life of many of those caring for loved ones at home, when it all becomes too much to cope with on your own.

Eventually, we began to struggle to fulfil Mum's needs and it was obvious extra assistance was required, so we enlisted the help of a local care company. We carried out research and opted for one that was reasonably priced with good reviews, although, to be honest, choice was limited. The installation of a key safe allowed carers to come and go easily and Mum reluctantly agreed to allow people into her home to help her with washing, dressing, medication and meals. It also meant someone would be popping in to check on her regularly, when we couldn't be there, and ensure she had some human interaction during the day. We were in contact with her every day, by phone or in person, and felt optimistic the new arrangement could work.

As Mum's health deteriorated, and she wasn't able to go out as much, she came to rely on the TV more and more (and we certainly knew about it if it ever went wrong!). When we visited, we would try to stimulate her mentally through conversation, discussing current events and stories in the news. We also played card games or encouraged her with her knitting, which she enjoyed, although stiff, arthritic fingers made this increasingly difficult. However, dealing with everyday practicalities meant time was always short. We hoped that with her immediate needs being met by carers, we would have more time just to sit and chat, but the carers did not work out as well as we hoped and there were many problems.

Early in 2016, we were granted Power of Attorney

(POA) to relieve Mum of some of the day-to-day decision making which she now found so confusing. There are two types of Lasting Power of Attorney (LPA): health and welfare, and property and financial affairs. You can apply for one or both types online via the UK government website (there is a charge for each type) or appoint a solicitor to set this up on your behalf. As employing a solicitor can be expensive, we decided to do this ourselves and found the process to be relatively straightforward. It is worth noting that this needs to be arranged when the person it concerns still has mental capacity to agree, otherwise LPA may not be awarded, so it is worth thinking ahead.

We now had overall responsibility for Mum's medication. In the early days, this meant collecting prescriptions from the doctor's surgery, taking them to the chemist and then going back for the various medicines. Later, the doctor's surgery would send prescriptions directly to the pharmacy but this didn't always work as well as we would have liked and involved lots of phone calls and chasing up. Once collected, tablets were transferred to a pill organiser, ready to be given by the carers at the appropriate time. This subsequently changed to blister packs, made up by the pharmacist, so that it was easy to administer the necessary medication at the correct time.

At this point, Mum was on a lot of medication ranging from painkillers to manage her arthritis (and, later, morphine patches) to a weekly tablet for osteoporosis which had to be taken in a certain way.

The carers were responsible for giving Mum her medication. However, there were many issues with this. They were supposed to visit four times a day, within a specified time slot, and record their movements in a logbook that was kept at the house. However, for one reason or another, visits were often not spaced as they should be.

Mum needed to be given her first doses of medication early and if the carer arrived late, Mum would be left in pain. It also meant that, if the next carer arrived early for the lunchtime visit, the medication would not be spaced correctly, and so on through the day.

Initially, the day's pills/blister packs were left on the table with the logbook, for easy access, but when Mum started to take the medication herself because she was in so much pain - which meant no one knew the exact time it had been taken - we had to move them out of reach. This also meant that they might be ignored by a new carer who was unfamiliar with Mum's routine, even though it was clearly stated in her care manual. If, as happened sometimes, a carer would miss a visit, again Mum would be left in pain and medication not properly spaced. The osteoporosis tablet had to be taken first thing in the morning, with a full glass of water, half an hour before food or drink, and in an upright position, but carers never had the time to supervise this correctly. More often than not, Mum would be given all of her tablets together, the one for osteoporosis included, washed down with tea after she had had breakfast.

When morphine patches were introduced to ease the unforgiving pain of chronic arthritis, they had to be changed every few days but even though the date was recorded on both the patch and in the care manual, carers would often forget. On occasion, they wouldn't remove the old patch or change it too soon. This was a controlled drug and Mum could only be prescribed so many at a time. We would carefully crosscheck the date on the patch against those remaining in the box and count the number of days in between. Mistakes were often found to have been made by inexperienced carers given responsibility for administering this tightly controlled drug.

On one occasion, a carer accidentally gave Mum an overdose of strong pain-relieving medicine. It was Saturday. Fish and chip day. One of us would always go to the local fish shop and buy Mum's favourite cod and chips for lunch. When we arrived, Mum seemed groggy and not her usual self. On checking the blister pack, we discovered that two doses of painkillers had been taken within a short period of time. A paramedic was called to check Mum over and we then sat with her to wait it out, until the effects had worn off. It transpired that the carer on duty had made a serious mistake by not checking the times recorded in the care manual.

This was not uncommon. Visits were supposed to be recorded with details of medication given and a comment on Mum's general health that day. However, to complicate matters further, the carers would frequently record incorrect times. One carer in particular, whom we will call Joanne, used to enter times that were far from accurate to cover her tracks about the timing of visits. Mum was an unreliable witness and could not tell us what time carers had been there. This meant the times recorded for medication could not be relied on. Once we became aware of this dangerous practice, we began to monitor this carer's movements more closely. She would quite happily enter the wrong time, even when we were present so knew for certain she was lying about the timing of visits. Sometimes, she would leave the time blank and backfill on a subsequent visit. Although the worst offender, she wasn't the only carer to do this and carers, at that time, weren't able to log visits by phone meaning it was more difficult to check. We contacted the care company and, following a lengthy meeting at their office, they assured us that those responsible would be spoken to. Still, the problems continued.

To be fair, the carers were low paid, often poorly trained and under pressure. Incredibly, they did not get paid for the journey to and from clients making timekeeping even more difficult as they tried to plan the most economic and efficient route. We appreciate that it is a stressful job. In spite of this, some of the carers were efficient and kind, but many who were didn't stay in the role for long. Mum liked routine and familiar faces, so each new person coming in increased her anxiety and had to build up her trust. She was also uncomfortable having a man attend to her personal, sometimes intimate, needs, particularly a stranger. Later on, Mum would be looked after by some very competent male carers, who she liked and relied on a great deal, but at this time she didn't like the fact that a completely unknown man could just walk into her house without prior introduction. It was a constant concern to us, allowing people we didn't know into our mother's home, but the greatest betrayal would come from the aforementioned carer, Joanne, someone who had been in the job for some time and Mum knew well and trusted, with devastating results.

Dos and Don'ts

Do:

- Find out as much as you can about what to expect when your loved one receives a diagnosis of dementia, both now and in the future. There are many different forms of dementia that may manifest in a variety of ways and symptoms will be unique to the individual.
- Remember that everyone experiences dementia differently. Many people are able to live fulfilling and independent lives after a diagnosis of dementia. Be patient and offer reassurance. Try to remain positive, even if you feel anxious or stressed, and do not allow your own concerns to transmit to your loved one.

Don't:

- Be afraid to ask for help and find out what assistance is available in your area (see the Useful Contacts section at the back of this book).
- Get angry or frustrated with your loved one if they are forgetful or repeat themselves as this will only add to their fear and confusion.

Facts and Figures

- At the beginning of 2023, around 900,000 people in the UK had some form of dementia, and this number is expected to rise sharply in the coming years (Alzheimer's Society).
- The most common forms of dementia are Alzheimer's disease, vascular dementia, Lewy body dementia, frontotemporal dementia and mixed dementia. Alzheimer's disease is the most common form of dementia and accounts for around 60% of diagnoses in the UK (Dementia UK).

Chapter 2
Jeanie with the Light Brown Hair

Mum was born on the 18th of December, 1924, in Walsall, in what is now the West Midlands, to parents Hannah and Clarence Morgan. She was to be one of six children having four brothers and a sister. Ken was the eldest, then Joan, Arnold, Mum (Jean), Jim, and youngest brother, Cyril.

Throughout their lives the two sisters were known as Joan and Jean, although they were christened Vera and Nancy respectively. Mum hated the name Nancy and never used it. Two of her brothers, Arnold and Jim, also went by their middle names, so this was not uncommon in their family.

As a child, Mum spent a simple but happy childhood, growing up with her brothers and sister to whom she was always very close. The two girls would go down to the local park and join in with their brothers and their friends, playing rounders and cricket. Later they learnt to play tennis and sometimes visited the local ice rink, where they wobbled round the edge, only to discover their eldest brother, Ken, was a natural, whizzing around on his skates and showing off.

The family lived in a tiny mid-terrace house in Field Road, Bloxwich. Space was tight in the traditional two up, two down property. Like many houses at that time, it had an outside toilet in the yard, where spiders and other creepy crawlies lurked, and no bathroom. There was a piano in the front parlour, although it was never clear how it came to be there and if anyone could play more than 'Chopsticks'. If they did, we girls never heard them during our many visits through the years.

There was a walk-in pantry in the back room and a small kitchen where our grandma would prepare family meals. She made the best chips, hand cut from potatoes and fried on the stove in an old-fashioned chip pan (there were no oven chips back then). Grandma also made thick and creamy custard with sterilised milk, which was delicious.

Our granddad, Clarence, would return home each evening to be greeted by the waiting family, black with coal dust after working long, hard hours down the nearby coal mine in the 'Black Country' that would eventually claim his life. Every evening he would strip off his dirty clothes and wash in the tin bath in front of the fire, filled by water heated on the stove. Sadly, he could not wash away the coal dust he had been breathing in all day, infecting his lungs. He later suffered a horrible death from coal workers' Pneumoconiosis (known as CWP or black lung disease) which can occur through continuous exposure to coal dust, irreparably damaging the lungs. It probably didn't help that he smoked, but it was much more common in those days before people knew how bad it was for you. He used to save up Player's cigarette cards out of the packets for his grandchildren to collect.

Mum was an intelligent girl, who was good at English, but had to leave school, aged fourteen, to contribute to the family budget. Career choices were limited and she considered herself lucky to get a job at a local greengrocer's where Joan was already working. The sisters hated the spiders that used to come in the boxes of bananas from overseas and, on one occasion, Joan was terrified to discover what she believed to be a tarantula walking up the wall. The job was close to home and paid a reasonable wage, so there were no travel costs, ideal as the sisters gave almost all of their wages to our grandma. But they were happy enough and the future stretched ahead, full of possibility. However, within a very short time the country would be at war, bringing an end to many of their dreams and aspirations.

At the start of the Second World War, Mum's brother, Ken, signed up and his brothers each joined the forces, as soon as they became old enough, radically changing the way of life for everyone. Mum used to recall many stories, some sad of losing close friends, some of happy reunions. One story, in particular, she told us about herself, aged sixteen, being rushed to hospital and operated on during an air raid. Her appendix had burst causing peritonitis. What a terrifying experience that must have been! Then, when fully recovered, she went to work in Crabtree's factory in Walsall, making gas masks and munitions, again alongside her sister, as everyone was expected to contribute to the war effort. Although the work was hard, there was a great sense of camaraderie at the factory with the young men and girls frequently playing pranks on one another.

As she grew into her teenage years Mum soon became very popular, especially with the boys. Her love of dancing and life, and her beautiful smile, won everyone over, earning her the nickname 'Smiler'. Mum had lovely brown hair that fell in soft curls down to her shoulders, often prompting friends to break into a chorus of 'Jeanie with the Light Brown Hair' (Stephen Foster, New York 1854).

During the war she met Bert (Albert) who was on leave from the RAF and based at Cosford, northwest of nearby Wolverhampton. Bert came from an army family, based in South East England where his father had been stationed at a seaside barracks. Dad was born in the army hospital (now a pub) and spent his early years amongst the soldiers and their families. It was here he developed a love of horses and learned to ride. Bert had one brother, Kenneth (Ken), who suffered from haemophilia, and would sadly die from this condition four years after the war ended. Our paternal grandad, Bert and Ken's dad, was a strict disciplinarian (although Grandma was more of a soft touch) and Dad loved to spend time with Mum's easy-going, noisy family in the Midlands who made him feel so welcome.

In 1943, after a short courtship, Mum and Dad married at a chapel in Bloxwich. Mum looked stunning in her simple white lace dress next to Dad in his RAF uniform. The wedding almost didn't take place as Joan's husband, Frank, took Dad to the wrong church, but they realised their mistake when the vicar shook his head and said there was no wedding booked for that day, and they arrived at the right chapel just in time. The celebrations had to be scaled down, due to rationing, but our maternal grandma saved up her ration coupons to provide a modest wedding breakfast. Joan, of course, was matron of honour and it was a happy occasion in spite of the war. According to Mum, people lived each day to the full, knowing it could very well be their last.

They didn't have the luxury of a honeymoon as it was too expensive and, besides, there was a war on, although Mum has told us that she and Dad managed to sneak off for a few days in Blackpool. Dad was in trouble with his superiors when he returned, being late to report back for duty. Immediately after, Dad was sent to fight in Italy. Mum would talk to us about agonising goodbyes, where she would leave Dad on a railway platform after trying to push him into an overcrowded train, packed with soldiers on their way to war. Many would not return to see their loved ones again. Our maternal grandma was extremely fortunate as, against the odds, all of her sons who were in service returned home.

Dad was a practical man, good with his hands, and trained as a mechanical engineer in the RAF, repairing motor vehicles (later on, he would always open the bonnet and repair his own cars – and ours, although he often despaired that we couldn't tell a gasket from a big end). He also loved driving, for which he received awards, and was so proud when, years later, he was able to drive a brand-new car from the showroom for the first and only time. It was a Russian manufactured Moskvitch; extremely safe but heavy to drive. Dad loved that car!

While Dad was away during the war, long letters were all that filled the intervening weeks and months between leave. Most of the time, Mum had no idea exactly where Dad was or when she might see him again (he was sent to Egypt for a time, as well as Italy). We still have some of the lovely letters they wrote to one another.

Mum remained in the Midlands with her parents and family until Dad returned home, eventually moving to South East England after the war to live with her in-laws, Walter and Violet ('Vi'), in the road she would call home for the next seventy years.

Chapter 3
Falls and Consequences

Like many elderly people living alone, the risk of Mum having a fall was real and ever present. In fact, she was to have three major falls from 2010 to the end of 2015, with the latter ones having more serious outcomes. Unfortunately, she would not escape the pain and trauma of stays in hospital and broken bones. This would, ultimately, decide her fate.

The first fall, in 2010, resulted in a fracture of the left humerus (upper arm). After a short stay in hospital, Mum was sent to a local rehabilitation centre (Rehab 1) for a short period to recover. The centre was clean, efficient and well run but Mum hated it from the outset, and keenly felt the loss of independence. All she wanted was to go back home where it felt safe and familiar and she couldn't understand why this wasn't possible.

'I'm so glad you're here. You can help me to pack.'

'Why, Mum, where are you going?'

'What do you mean "where am I going?" - home of course.'

'No, Mum, not for a little while.'

'Why not? What am I doing here?'

'To give you a rest while you get stronger.'

'Why? There's nothing wrong with me.'

'You've hurt your arm and need to give it time to mend.'

'I'm so glad you're here. You can help me to pack. I want to go home.'

'No, Mum, not just yet.'

'Yes, this afternoon, you can take me.'

'No, not today, but very soon.'

Ten minutes later she would ask the same thing and we would repeat the conversation. We visited every day, but even though it was a relatively short period, it felt like a long time to Mum before she was deemed fit enough to return home.

When Mum first left rehab, a care team was put in place by the NHS, free of charge. They were fantastic (which shows it can be done); efficient, reliable, pleasant and very good with Mum. Unfortunately, they were only able to provide assistance for up to six weeks, and after that we had to rely on the services of a private care company which Mum had to pay for.

This marked the start of a very difficult period for us, as we struggled to meet the increasing demands of a person living with dementia, while managing our own homes, families, jobs and lives. We were always busy, and effectively managing another household meant there was an endless list of practical things to be done, and someone had to oversee Mum's care at all times to ensure that her needs were always met. We both had files full of information as we divided up responsibility for dealing with particular aspects of Mum's life. Increasingly, we had less time for social visits, just to sit and chat with her, as there was always something pressing to be organised or dealt with that demanded our attention.

Mum continued to live at home with extra help until 2014 when she had a second, more serious fall. We had, by this time, installed a personal alarm system linked to her phone. Mum wore a 'panic button' round her neck that she could push to alert someone if she needed help. The alarm went through to a call centre and they would phone one of us, and alert the emergency services if needed. The carers were supposed to check that Mum was wearing this call button at all times, but often forgot. However, on this particular day, the system worked as it was supposed to and we were duly alerted that Mum had fallen.

On this occasion, she broke the neck of the femur (thigh bone) and a dynamic hip screw had to be fitted. This resulted in a long, painful wait in casualty and a much longer stay in hospital. Once settled, Mum didn't seem to mind being in the busy hospital ward. She was comfortable and well-looked after, and the nurses could monitor and control her pain. However, as soon as she was medically fit, she was discharged, owing to the constant pressure for beds. There followed a brief stay in a care home, when the hospital forgot to tell us that Mum had been moved, or where to, and there was a period of panic while we tried to track her down.

Then, shortly after, it was back to Rehab 1 for a period of rest, recuperation and physiotherapy.

Mum had a pleasant, light, spacious, single occupancy room at the front of the building. Again, she hated it. Our mum had always been very sociable and we thought she would enjoy having company and people of her own age to talk to but she refused to join in with activities or engage with anyone.

The seats in the lounge were arranged in a semi-circle around the television but Mum was rarely able to watch her favourite programmes and soaps. Certain individuals would hog the TV remote control and Mum didn't like to ask if they would change the channel. Between us, we visited daily, sometimes twice a day, but Mum was most unhappy when it was time for us to go, begging us not to leave her there. We felt terrible but there was no alternative, as she needed constant care and physio. She was also starting to rely on us more and more. We loved her and were happy to support her but began to question how we might manage in the future.

The physio sessions were tough but helped to make Mum stronger and get her back on her feet. We were impressed by both the efficiency and effectiveness of the treatment she received. In all, she stayed at Rehab 1 for around six weeks but was overjoyed when the time came for us to take her home. Physically, Mum was on the mend, but her mental capacity continued to deteriorate and symptoms, such as forgetfulness, worsened. We would make an arrangement with her and she would ring us back, sometimes immediately afterwards, often more than once, for us to explain what was happening. In November 2014, she went for an MRI scan to find out what was going on in her brain. When Mum was diagnosed with Alzheimer's disease in January 2015, it was not a surprise.

Around this time, we were introduced to a community specialist dementia nurse. We will never forget our first meeting. She was tall and slim, and heavily made-up with long, bleached blonde hair, dressed in bright pink trousers and a matching top. We were not at all optimistic that this was the right person to help us. We were so wrong! And we quickly learnt not to judge someone by their appearance.

This particular community nurse turned out be efficient, knowledgeable and a fierce advocate for Mum and our family. She correctly identified that Mum was suffering from low mood, as a result of dementia, and recommended the appropriate medication. Once Mum started on a mild antidepressant and something to help her sleep, her mood improved and she was more able to find joy in life again. The nurse also helped us to secure the things we needed to continue to care for Mum at home. Later, she would help to steer us through the tricky first steps of finding and securing a place in a care home.

Then, in September 2016, Mum had the fall that would change everything. Mum had been a little unwell for a day or so with diarrhoea and stomach cramps, and we had been backwards and forwards to her home to check on her, dealing with soiled clothes, changing bedclothes and encouraging her to drink so she didn't become dehydrated. At this time, Joanne was the main carer who attended the house and between us, we took care of Mum.

After a couple of days, it was apparent Mum wasn't improving, although she was drinking and even eating a little. It was the weekend and difficult to contact the doctor, so when we left that afternoon, we decided to call an ambulance if there was no change by the following morning. Joanne was due to go in to attend to Mum that evening and promised to phone us with an update when she arrived.

The phone call never came. For some reason, Joanne did not return to check on Mum. Instead, we were alerted by the personal alarm company that Mum had fallen. By the time we arrived, it was late evening. Mum was lying on the floor in an extremely distressed state. We couldn't risk trying to move her in case any bones had been broken and made Mum as comfortable as possible until the emergency services arrived. The attending paramedics, who were lovely, felt Mum needed to go into hospital to be checked out.

When asked later, Joanne said that she had been in to see Mum a little earlier than usual but forgotten to call. She said she had helped Mum undress and put on nightclothes and made her comfortable in bed. However, the bed had obviously not been slept in. Mum had also fallen in the lounge, not the bedroom, and was fully dressed in the same clothes we had helped her change into earlier that day. Joanne stuck to her story and said Mum must have got up and changed back into her trousers and top. As, by this point, Mum was unable to dress and undress without help, this seemed unlikely. There was no corresponding entry in the logbook but Joanne insisted she had just forgotten to write it up. We were saddened by her apparent betrayal of trust but had other pressing concerns to address.

The hospital was busy and we waited for some time with the ambulance crew, who were fantastic throughout, talking to Mum and reassuring her. When we were finally admitted to A&E, a young, obviously stressed, junior doctor shouted questions at Mum who was, by this time, very confused and in no fit state to answer. We politely explained that Mum suffered from Alzheimer's disease and could she please address her questions to us so we could help Mum to understand what was being asked. This was done, but made us wonder about the lack of training in dealing with dementia patients at that time. It was the first time we experienced such inappropriate handling of someone with dementia. Sadly, it would not be the last.

On this occasion, it was discovered that Mum had an impacted bowel, and she was admitted to a ward. She was in a weakened state, because of the sickness, and confused and frightened. We stayed with her that long night, holding her hand and repeatedly reassuring her.

Mum remained in hospital for a few days. Again,

beds were in short supply and it was agreed that she would go into rehab. This time Rehab 1 didn't have space, so an alternative was found. We had asked the hospital to dress Mum, ready for the move, but not to put her into a wheelchair until the taxi was ready to transport her as it caused her discomfort. A nurse was due to accompany her in the wheelchair taxi and we arranged to meet them at the care facility. We were the first to arrive, and were told by the care home manager that they were expecting two new arrivals, but had only agreed to take one. We waited and, sure enough, a taxi arrived from the hospital. It didn't contain Mum. The lady was greeted and wheeled inside.

Less than five minutes later, Mum arrived in another taxi. The accompanying nurse got out and was informed by the care home manager that they didn't have room for another patient. We protested, and so did the nurse, but to no avail. Meanwhile, Mum was left hunched over in a wheelchair in the taxi becoming increasingly uncomfortable and anxious. She sat there for the best part of an hour while the nurse phoned the hospital and argued with the manager of the care facility. Eventually, realising Mum was now in severe pain and distress, the nurse ordered the taxi to return to the hospital.

We followed in our own cars but, by the time we had parked, we had no idea where in the hospital Mum had been taken and there was no sign of the taxi. It transpired that she had been admitted to a different ward. When we eventually tracked her down, Mum was in a very agitated state. She was made comfortable in bed and the senior nurse on the ward promised there would be a full investigation. The next day Mum was moved to a different rehabilitation facility (Rehab 2). We eventually received an apology from the hospital, although no one ever admitted liability for the mistake, with the home and hospital each blaming the other. Like many future occasions, it did nothing to help our mum.

So, moving on again. Rehab 2 was in a pleasant situation, close to both Kim's home and the seafront. Within a short while of being there, Mum seemed to tolerate the wheelchair a little better, thus enabling more trips out. During her stay, some of her grandchildren were happy to take her out for a walk along the seafront and treat her to her favourite ice cream.

Rehab 2 had much to commend it. Once again, Mum didn't take to it for some reason. But it was clean and well-organised with pleasant, helpful staff. The facility had another major asset; a consistently smiling, but persuasive physiotherapist, who was brilliant at his job. Within the few weeks that Mum was living at Rehab 2, she was up on her feet and walking confidently, up and down the tricky, sloping floors of the upper level where her room was situated. With the aid of her trusty walking frame of course! It was the strongest and steadiest we had seen her for some time. It confirmed our belief that gentle physical activity was essential to the well-being and physical capability of the elderly. The physiotherapist was just what Mum needed; patient but firm and he quickly built up her confidence. He also gave us exercises to do with Mum while sitting in her chair to help strengthen and support her neck, which we continued to do for as long as we were able after she was discharged. It shows what can be done with the right kind of care.

However, her mental state was not so good. While she was staying at Rehab 2, Mum's mind seemed to play tricks on her, as a result of Alzheimer's, and she couldn't remember where she was or why she was there. Coupled with the fact she had taken a dislike to the place, this created many problems. We would be called out more than once.

On one particular evening, the carer on duty was having trouble persuading Mum to take her medication. We went over to discover a wild-eyed Mum, shouting at the poor carer, which was most out of character. And this time there was no calming her down.

'Who are you?' Mum said, suspiciously.

'It's me, your daughter.'

'Thank goodness. They're trying to poison me.'

'No, Mum, they're not, they're trying to help. It's to make you feel better.'

'Who are you?'

'I'm your daughter.'

'You're not, you're an imposter. If you were my daughter, you wouldn't be helping them. They're trying to poison me. Someone, please, help me!'

There was no reasoning with her, and it was very upsetting. However, it was one of the very few times Mum didn't fully recognise one of us. Throughout the entire bumpy, messy, frightening journey ahead, thankfully, Mum continued to know who we were. We were always 'her Sue and Kim'; her precious daughters. Sadly, this is not the case for everyone in the later stages of dementia.

Dos and Don'ts

Do:

- Expect things to change. Dementia is a progressive illness and you will need to regularly assess how well your loved one is coping and constantly re-evaluate their needs.
- Remain flexible. An arrangement that works well early on in a diagnosis of dementia might not do so at a later stage.

Don't:

- Forget to carry out a regular risk assessment if your loved one is living at home by themselves. As far as possible, remove potential hazards and consider installing handrails and grab rails. Look into ways they can prepare meals and drinks safely or consider using a meal delivery service.

Facts and Figures

- One in three people over the age of sixty-five fall at least once a year (Age UK).
- Nearly 100,000 older people (aged 65+) suffered hip fractures in 2017/18 (NHS Digital).
- Having a fall is a major source of worry for older people in the UK, with 4.3 million (36%) citing this as their biggest concern (Age UK).

Chapter 4
Sadness and Joy

The house we grew up in was a modest, three-bedroomed semi, which Mum and Dad shared with our paternal grandparents and Dad's brother, Ken. It was, perhaps, a little less crowded than the house in Bloxwich but Mum still did not have the luxury of her own home and shared kitchen space with her mother-in-law. There was no central heating and every day in the winter months Mum would get up early, creeping through the freezing house, to lay and light the fire in the grate so it was warm and cosy when the family got up. This continued for many years and we can both remember sitting by the fire as children, reading and warming our toes (ignoring warnings about chilblains).

Life was never to be easy for Mum. It must have been difficult for her, moving away from her close-knit family to begin a new life over a hundred and fifty miles away. Very few people had telephones at that time so Mum must have felt quite isolated, particularly in the early days. However, her sunny disposition meant she quickly made new friends, many who remained a part of Mum's life for years. Lasting friendships were forged with neighbours and workmates alike.

Coming from a large and loving family, Mum longed to have children of her own. She adored babies and hoped to have a big family, but, unfortunately, this would never happen.

A short time after the move to the seaside, Mum was happy to fall pregnant with her first baby. However, joy was to turn to sadness a few months later. In July, 1947, Mum gave birth prematurely to a little boy who weighed no more than a bag of sugar. He must have inherited Mum's strong will as he fought hard to live, surviving for nine days. He slept in a shoebox, carefully placed in the top drawer of a chest of drawers, with a hot water bottle to keep him warm. There were no incubators or premature baby units at that time. In the short time he lived, our brother was christened Michael.

Sadly, there was little support for mothers who had lost their babies back then and our brother wasn't even afforded his own funeral and was, instead, buried in an adult grave with a stranger who had passed away around the same time. All our parents had was a plot number with someone else's name on the headstone. There was also no grief counselling or therapy and, for the most part, Mum had to deal with her painful emotions on her own. Such matters weren't openly discussed back then. That and subsequent losses would remain with Mum for the rest of her life. We cannot imagine what she went through and it was only later in life, when we had our own children, that we could begin to understand the depth of this tragedy. Thankfully, things are very different today and such loss is recognised and mothers are better supported in their grief.

Shortly afterwards, to everyone's delight, Mum fell pregnant again and gave birth to a healthy baby girl named Susan. Not wanting Susan, who everyone has always called Sue, to be their only child, Mum and Dad would try again and again to expand their small family. Yet more tragedy followed with two stillborn babies, both boys, and further miscarriages. Then, after a long gap of fourteen years, to the family's great relief and happiness, Mum and Dad were blessed with another daughter, Kim. So we sisters (co-authors of this book) had arrived.

With fourteen years between us, effectively growing up as only children, it is surprising that we are close, but the bond has grown stronger over the years, particularly since our fight for Mum began. And, although we didn't have other brothers and sisters, we had many cousins in the Midlands and looked forward to our holidays spent with them.

Our childhood memories of Bloxwich will be remembered forever. We would travel with Mum and Dad and stay at Grandma's house in Field Road for as long as we were able. We would meet up with aunts, uncles and cousins at local parks and carry on the family tradition of playing rounders and cricket. Cannock Chase and Walsall Arboretum were among our favourite places to visit. It was not uncommon for us to have a go at boating on a nearby lake. On occasion, we would travel further afield to Dovedale, in the Peak District, and there are many photos of us crossing the stepping stones on the River Dove. Wherever we were, blankets would go down and baskets would come out filled with all sorts of treats for a picnic. They were wonderful times!

We would then return to Field Road, tired but full of the day's fun and memories. All the families gathered round an enormous table which took up most of Grandma's back room. We would talk, laugh, play cards and sing. And our large extended family loved to sing, a talent that has, unfortunately, bypassed us. Sometimes, Mum would even try to muster up a tune on the piano mentioned earlier.

Mum's sister, our Aunt Joan, was married to Frank. They were a generous, funny, friendly couple, loved by all. Sadly, they never had children, a great shame as they would have been fantastic parents. Coming from such a large family, the couple had many nephews and nieces, so they always made a huge fuss of us and our cousins. Many holidays were spent with Joan and Frank in Wales or Devon and they would often come to stay with us at the seaside. They were everyone's favourite aunt and uncle, devoted to each other until the day they died in their eighties, within a few short months of one another. Mum and Joan had a dream of moving to Wales and opening a guest house. It's a pity it never came to pass. They would have made excellent landladies.

Chapter 5
Care Home 1

During her stay at Rehab 2, in October 2016, it was agreed by the family and Social Services that Mum needed more care. It was felt that she could no longer live safely at home on her own, even with additional support. Reluctantly, we put it to her that she consider moving to a home where she could be cared for round the clock. During a meeting with the aforementioned community dementia nurse specialist, on one of Mum's better days when her understanding was greater, we broached the subject. Mum seemed to agree this was a good idea and said she would be happy to give it a try. We then began the process of looking for a suitable care home.

It was our understanding that we would have a choice and we carried out an initial search online for those homes in the area with good reviews and a high rating from the CQC. We then followed up the ones on our shortlist with a visit. We had to make an appointment to see some of the homes but others invited us to turn up unannounced as long as we avoided meal times. This gave us a sense that they had nothing to hide (not that the others did, of course).

A couple of homes looked promising but we

discounted one as the corridors were narrow and cluttered and we wondered how Mum would fare navigating around with her walking frame. Two of the homes seemed busy and the residents were happily taking part in activities which was something we were keen on (in one, there was a rather ambitious project to cover balloons with papier mâché). It is extremely sad to see a line of elderly residents sitting in a row in front of the television with no other means of stimulation. At the homes we liked the staff were visible and actively interacting with residents. Unfortunately, no places were available at those we felt would best suit Mum's needs. So was it left to Social Services to allocate a home, and we put our trust in them to find Mum a suitable place to live.

Social Services put us in touch with Care Home 1, which had vacancies, and we made an appointment to view it. Back in those days, we were naïve and had less idea of what to look for and, with hindsight, we focussed on the wrong things. The way in which a home is run and managed is more important than cosmetic appearance.

On first impression, Care Home 1 gave us no immediate cause for concern. From the outside, the large, imposing building looked impressive. The then manager, whom we had met while Mum was in Rehab 2, seemed very pleasant, and greeted us warmly. Inside the home looked clean and the staff seemed friendly, although there were not many carers on duty.

The home was fairly small in size, with around

twelve residents, which we felt would suit Mum, and in a very good location. There was a lovely, large park nearby, full of mature trees (which Mum always loved) and ideal for taking Mum out in her wheelchair.

The vacant single occupancy room was on the first floor and there was a somewhat rickety lift just about big enough to accommodate a wheelchair and carer. (Later on, this lift would sometimes be out of order, stranding Mum and other residents upstairs for a couple of days or so.) The bedroom itself was a decent size, bright and overlooking the small garden, but we later realised it did not have a functional emergency cord or button.

Along the wide hall was what appeared to be a well-appointed bathroom, although there was no proper wet room and Mum would later find it upsetting being lowered in and out of the bath. Adjacent to this was a separate toilet for staff and visitors to use. There were two downstairs lounges each having a conservatory. The two residents' toilets had easy access, and there was a large kitchen. The residents we met on that day all seemed happy enough.

Mum was eventually discharged from Rehab 2 in early November, physically the strongest we had seen her for some time. The move to Care Home 1 went quite smoothly. We had arranged a wheelchair taxi to take Mum the short journey, and one of us went in the taxi with her while the other drove to her new home separately.

We hung much treasured photos around the walls and brought in her favourite ornaments to make her surroundings more familiar to her. We also took in a set of drawers which gave her additional space to keep her clothes and helped keep the room tidy. We moved Mum's electric armchair into the care home to make her more comfortable during the day, as the upright chairs provided in the lounge caused great discomfort and severe pain to her arthritic joints. As it was familiar, it also helped to make her feel more at home.

We spent as much time as we could with Mum and, although very anxious at first, she settled in and made friends with the other residents. In particular, she bonded with a lovely lady, Dot. She also became friends with a gentleman named Bob, and often when we visited we would find them sitting holding hands. Dot had one son who wasn't able to visit very often so we always included her in our conversations when we went in to see Mum. She, too, suffered from dementia and would often 'lose' her handbag and we would spend a good deal of time reassuring her that it had been under her chair all along.

It was always interesting, talking to the residents. You never knew what someone had achieved in their life and finding out about a person, and imagining the person they once were, could be a humbling experience. The residents had many stories to tell; maybe about the war, some had travelled, while others had enjoyed great success in their chosen career. Many had raised families and had children, grandchildren and great-children. Once you found the key to unlocking their memories, it was surprising what you might learn.

At that time, many of the carers were compassionate, caring and attentive and soon felt more like friends or extended family. There was one individual in particular, Stuart, who always did his best to help. He appeared to work long hours and was often on call, and The Owner appeared to rely on him a great deal. Mum liked Stuart and we trusted him to act in her best interests. If there were any issues to do with Mum and her care, he would listen to what we had to say and try to resolve matters. However, as we were soon to discover, some of these friendly, familiar faces could, and did, leave without warning or explanation, and this eventually included Stuart.

When someone has care and support needs, such as in a care home setting, a care plan is drawn up and agreed on. This includes the expectations of care that need to be met and hoped for outcomes. This should then be regularly reviewed, and at a minimum, yearly.

Early on, The Owner carried out an assessment of Mum. She wanted to routinely use the hoist to transfer her which horrified us, especially after all the hard work the rehab team had done to (quite literally) get her back on her feet. This was probably the period of time when Mum was physically strongest and steadiest on her feet.

To avoid this, Stuart agreed to work with Mum with the help of another carer, Vena, and they would encourage her to walk with her frame, gradually gaining her trust and building her confidence in a new setting. This also gave her some independence when needing to go to the toilet. We felt more relaxed when we knew these two particular carers were on duty and were happy to leave Mum in their capable care.

We always had a more enjoyable experience when Vena was on duty, as she was pleasant, bubbly, kind and chatty. She would speak to us about her own culture and said she looked after the residents as if they were her own grandparents, and this was borne out by her interactions with them, which filled us with hope that Mum's time at the care home would be happy.

In the first few weeks of Mum being at the home, Social Services arranged a safeguarding meeting with us to assess Mum's mental capacity and ensure she wasn't being held against her will. This is standard practice. We were introduced to a social worker, who we'd never met before. It was obvious from the outset he seemed to think it was a complete waste of his time, and actually said as much. His abrupt manner and body language made it difficult to communicate with him effectively. He actually went so far as to say that he didn't approve of elderly relatives being placed in care, as he felt they would be better looked after at home by family. We were already feeling anxious and guilty about the move, and his attitude made us feel worse. But we had exhausted all other options by this point, and this seemed to be the only solution. However, the necessary paperwork had to be completed, and the right boxes had to be ticked, so we pressed on and kept quiet. With hindsight, we should have reported him to Social Services, but this was a new and scary world to us and we didn't want to do anything that might negatively impact Mum.

Around this time, we had to make a decision about Mum's house, and decided to rent it out. There were good reasons to do this. Firstly, it seemed morally wrong for the house to remain empty when it could be of use to someone who needed it, and it ultimately fulfilled this purpose for several years, becoming home to a family with three children. Secondly, if she asked, we could genuinely tell Mum that her house was still there and she always had the option to move back if things didn't work out. Lastly, it has to be said that living in a care home does not come cheap, and as Mum owned her own house she was required to contribute to the cost, but more about that later.

In late December, Care Home 1 arranged a Christmas carol concert to which family and friends were invited. It was not particularly well attended and it saddened us that many residents didn't appear to have visitors, even at Christmas. But we joined in enthusiastically, if not exactly tunefully. Everyone seemed to be in good spirits, although the manager seemed to be a little quiet. Then, later that afternoon, to our surprise, she came round to everyone to say goodbye. We were a little taken aback, as there had been no mention of her leaving, and we felt a little uneasy about her sudden departure, but wished her the best. No explanation was given by her or The Owner.

Sunday, the 18th of December was Mum's 92nd birthday. Being a non-working day, the family arranged to meet up at the home. An extra-large birthday cake was made to make sure there was enough for all the residents to have a slice. We also baked two large plates of cupcakes just in case we ran short or there were additional visitors that day. There were banners, cards, flowers and lots of birthday presents but, most of all, Mum enjoyed being with her family, surrounded by love.

Exactly one week later, on Christmas Day, we brought Mum home to have Christmas dinner with her family. Such an undertaking required a lot of planning to ensure everything went smoothly and we had everything necessary to care for Mum for a short time. This included medication, a change of clothes, her walking frame, and a safety frame for the downstairs toilet. One of us went to the care home to help get Mum ready and waited for the pre-booked wheelchair taxi. We then travelled the short journey with Mum to join the family. What a precious few hours we had but, all too quickly, the time had gone and the taxi arrived to take Mum back. She returned to the home full of turkey and sprouts, Christmas pudding and mince pies, laden with more gifts, but best of all were the wonderful memories we had of a truly happy day.

Early in 2017, a new manager was appointed at Care Home 1. She seemed pleasant and soon settled into her new role, but would often seem tense or stressed and there never seemed to be enough staff on duty, particularly at weekends, which was a concern.

As previously mentioned, one of the most noticeable differences between homes when we had initially been looking for a suitable place for Mum was how the residents occupied their time. In some homes, it was disappointing to witness rows of elderly women and men slumped in chairs with the television on in the corner, but no one watching, and no outside space. In the better run homes, daily activities were organised and there was a garden where residents could sit outside when the weather allowed. Care Home 1, at this time, probably fell between the two, with a small garden residents could make use of and enjoy and some activities.

In the beginning, there was a list of that week's activities on the wall, but these rarely seemed to happen. We took this up with the manager and, for a short time, the home employed someone specifically to oversee activities. In theory, this was a good idea but often she would be called away for other duties, leaving willing visitors to continue in whatever way they could. We would find ourselves encouraging residents to roll a ball at skittles or take part in a quiz – often coming up with surprisingly cheeky answers. They joined in according to their abilities and were always good sports and lots of fun, so we never minded helping out.

One activity involved the residents trying to guess

a particular smell (such as lavender, lemon or vinegar), while blindfolded. This kind of activity can help to stimulate the part of the brain that triggers memories and certain scents can aid recall. For example, the aroma of certain herbs might lead Mum to remember her garden or cooking in her kitchen at home. There was also a memory board whereby residents would look at a tray of objects for a while before it was taken away and they were asked to remember the contents.

The activities coordinator was well-intentioned and did what she could with a virtually non-existent budget. She was also friendly and, as we visited often, we would naturally chat to her. It was from her we first heard about 'sundowning', a distressing condition that affects some people suffering from dementia, who can become hyperactive, agitated and confused, especially at night, causing sleep disruption, although we weren't aware that this was ever a problem with Mum.

Then, when we visited one day, we found out that this individual had left suddenly for unknown reasons. From then on activities became much more sporadic. Later on, a member of staff took on the role of promoting the home on social media and someone would whip out a camera to document an activity, such as singing or dancing, when initiated. But it often seemed to us that, no sooner had they taken a photo or short video, the activity would be brought to an end.

We bought books and magazines into the home to share with Mum. She was never a big reader during her life, but always liked magazines and enjoyed it when we read to her, particularly short stories. We also compiled photograph albums to look through with her. This proved to be very successful, as the images often triggered memories about people and places that were important. The home would often play DVDs, and certain favourites in particular. To this day, we can recite particular films, word for word.

When Mum first arrived at the home, meals were prepared by a jovial lady who was employed solely to do the cooking and, for a while, the residents enjoyed home cooked meals. Unfortunately, she left due to ill health, so food was then prepared by one of the carers on duty and this did not always look so appetising.

The standard menu included a choice of cereal or toast for breakfast. Dinner, served at lunchtime, usually consisted of a cooked meal, meat and two veg, followed by a dessert of some kind. Then, later, there would be sandwiches, salad and maybe a piece of cake. They had biscuits in between with a cup of tea. The latter was a great favourite of many of the residents, especially Bob, who could always find room for biscuits and cake. Mum always enjoyed her food and this, to us, was a good sign.

During the spring and summer we spent as much time as we could with Mum, taking her out whenever possible to the local park. Although it was only a short distance Mum could just about tolerate the journey in her wheelchair. On a bad day, arthritis would cause severe pain in her joints which was made unbearable by the bumps and ruts in the path. On these occasions, which happened more and more frequently, we would have to turn back as the pain was too much for her. On a good day, when we managed to get her there, she would enjoy an ice cream, followed by a cup of tea and being pushed around the lovely gardens. Every other weekend, different bands would play in the bandstand in the centre of the park, which always attracted crowds, and Mum enjoyed this on the occasions we were able to take her. Back at the home, weather permitting, the carers would occasionally take out a comfortable chair so Mum was able to sit in the garden for a while with some of the other residents.

During the warmer months, the home organised a barbeque. Residents' families were invited to join in and sausages and burgers were served. Stuart acted as DJ and would get the residents singing and tapping their feet in time with the music. He also liked to tell jokes which caused a lot of fun and hilarity especially as visiting families' children would sit in the front and chip in with the punchline. But it was all taken in good part.

Towards the end of 2017, the then manager left suddenly. Again, no explanation was offered for her departure. There then followed a period when there was a more rapid turnover of staff and the atmosphere at the home felt much more unsettled. We would be introduced to new carers and then never see them again. Staff in other areas, such as admin, also left unexpectedly without explanation. The home didn't have a constant, stable base of staff and there was often a tense atmosphere.

New, inexperienced or untrained staff were a concern as we often had to remind them to take care when handling Mum due to her comorbidities. Sometimes she would shout out in pain when they took her to the toilet. As this frequently occurred in front of us, it made us worry about how she was being handled when we weren't there. While we don't think anyone intentionally meant to hurt Mum, she needed to be treated very gently.

By this point, Stuart seemed to be around much less and Vena had left to pursue a career as a nurse (and a great asset to the profession she would be). Many of the new carers, although pleasant enough, were not known to us or Mum. Sometimes we would arrive to find the carers on duty in the garden smoking and chatting, meaning there was often no one available in the home to look after residents. At this time, Mum's chair was situated in the second, smaller lounge with Dot and Bob. For some reason, the carers seemed to check on them less than those seated in the main lounge, possibly because the main lounge was close to the office and kitchen. When we visited we felt there were never enough carers around to properly keep an eye on vulnerable residents.

Mum would sometimes describe strange and concerning incidents that had happened to her at the home. At first, we put this down to confusion due to dementia. However, sometimes she would be adamant that she had been mistreated in some way. On one particular occasion, she told us she had been roughly handled and left alone, cold and frightened, after wetting the bed. Mum told us the night carer had been angry that she had had to strip and change the bed. Mum was very distressed and obviously traumatised by the incident, and described the carer who had been working that night in some detail. We reported this to the manager in charge at the time and discovered that the carer Mum had referred to had, indeed, been on duty that night and Mum had, unfortunately, wet the bed. Mum was extremely anxious saying she was scared in case she had another accident and the carer would shout at her again. After this, we were concerned that certain other things she told us might not be due to dementia.

We privately discussed the possibility of finding an alternative care home, but we knew how much Mum hated any change to her routine. Even moving her into the main lounge for an occasion such as a carol concert could make her quite upset and agitated about the unfamiliar surroundings. She liked being around Dot and felt comfortable with her and, of course, Bob. We were aware that Bob's family also had reservations and concerns about the home, but were afraid to complain for fear of reprisals, something we were also mindful of with Mum.

December came round and Mum's 93rd birthday. Being a Monday, most of the family were at work, nonetheless we went to the care home, arms laden with gifts, cards and, of course, a huge birthday cake.

Mum's favourite was homemade Victoria sponge. In her younger days she loved baking and made some delicious cakes. Fortunately, we both take after her in this respect, unlike singing!

Six days later, on the 24th of December, we again managed to take Mum out of the home for a few hours to celebrate an early Christmas. All the family, including grandchildren and great-grandchildren, was there to greet her, and gave her the fuss she so deserved. Christmas dinner was served with all the trimmings followed by the traditional Christmas pud, which was soaked in brandy and set light to. It was a happy day, but little did we realise this would be the last time Mum would be able to make the short journey across town to be with us all at Christmas.

Dos and Don'ts

Do:

- Visit care homes in your area to get an idea of what is available and the potential costs involved. This will also allow you to compare the different services to see which ones would be best suited to your relative. Prepare a list of questions beforehand and create a tick list for purposes of comparison.
- Think ahead. Care homes are often oversubscribed with long waiting lists, particularly the more popular ones, and it may be advisable to add your loved one's name to their list well in advance if you feel you may need their services in future.

Don't:

- Forget to regularly review the situation, even after your loved one has moved to a home, to see if your current arrangements are still in their best interests.
- Be afraid to consider your options, including moving your loved one, if things are no longer working at the current home. Sometimes a move might be the best option.

Facts and Figures

- As at August 2022, half a million people live in some kind of residential care (care and nursing homes) in the UK (Carehome.co.uk).

Chapter 6
Working Days

After the war, Dad found work as a milkman. Originally, his float was pulled by a horse, the most memorable being Daphne, who everyone used to pet and feed. She could be cantankerous at times but enjoyed being made a fuss of, and Dad was very fond of her.

Dad had a motorbike on which he used to ride to and from the dairy. When she was quite small, Sue loved to ride up and down the road on the bike with Dad, whenever she could sneak past Mum. Dad would sit her on a cushion between the handlebars, not something you can imagine doing these days, but they were different times in respect of health and safety.

Mum and Dad were still living with Walter and Vi (our paternal grandparents) but money was always tight. When Sue was small, Mum found employment doing domestic work for a family in an affluent local suburb. The employer thought a great deal of Mum and they soon formed a bond, becoming good friends. So, as a bonus, they let us use their beach hut situated along the seafront not far from our home. The beach hut was in a prime position on the beach and quickly became a family favourite for days out. We were lucky enough to spend many happy hours by the sea. Unfortunately, the employers later moved abroad. This left Mum out of work (and out of a beach hut!) so she then found work helping a school teacher with domestic chores. Hardworking and loyal, Mum was always well thought of and would, again, stay there for several years.

After Kim was born, Mum started working from home to supplement her income. The necessary jobs, which included weighing and bagging nails, would be delivered to our house and picked up when finished. With the help of Dad, between them they would weigh the nails on the scales provided and seal them in plastic bags. This was a long and tedious job which took many painstaking hours. Later, when Mum acquired an electric Singer sewing machine she turned her hand to making plastic pants for babies. These would fit snugly over the top of terry nappies to help prevent leaks as disposable nappies were largely unavailable back then.

When Kim grew older and settled in school, Mum went to work at a local factory, making electrical accessories. Like many women employed there, she had a part-time position and worked the morning shift so she could be home for the end of school. Mum loved the camaraderie of the factory floor and made several lasting friendships. She remained there until aged sixty, when company policy at that time dictated she had to retire.

However, Mum was not one to sit around idly and

wanted to supplement her pension. She was lucky enough to find work with a lovely lady, who needed extra help around the house as she suffered from multiple sclerosis. She lived in a large bungalow close to the seafront, and Mum would walk to and from work each day. Mum dedicated the next ten years or so to looking after this lady, long after Mum herself was advancing in years. Her energy has always amazed us.

During the course of her life, Mum had many jobs and always worked hard. If she needed anything for the home or family, she would save her money and refused to ever buy anything on credit even when it became more readily available. (Although we can remember her saving Green Shield Stamps to buy extras for the home.)

A few years later, when our grandparents passed away (Vi in 1970 and Walter a year later in 1971), Dad and Mum inherited the house. Dad would live there until a few weeks before his death in 2005 and Mum until she reached the point where she could no longer look after herself safely.

Chapter 7
Frustrations and Challenges

The year 2018 would prove to be one of our most challenging periods of dealing with the adult care sector. At the time, we thought we were doing the right thing by continuing to try and make things work. With hindsight, we would have been far better finding another home for Mum before things became really unworkable.

In many respects, Mum was one of the lucky ones as she had a loving family looking out for her. Many people living in care homes have no one, so when things go wrong there is nobody to speak up for them, something we became aware of throughout our experiences with the adult social care sector.

At the beginning of 2018, one or two new carers were employed, which was pleasing. With more staff on the ground, we thought maybe things would start to improve. How wrong could we be? It would prove to be a miserable year for us.

As a replacement manager had not yet been appointed, we began to have more direct dealings with the care home owner, and on the 19th of February we were invited to a review meeting about Mum. As well as ourselves and The Owner, also at the meeting, for reasons that were never made clear, was a lady who worked in the office upstairs.

At the meeting, we voiced our concerns about the constantly changing staff and reassurances were received from The Owner that the staffing situation was being addressed. We had begun to notice a deterioration in Mum's overall health and raised this with The Owner. It was then suggested that Mum be placed on the palliative care register. This alarmed and surprised us as no way did we consider she was anywhere near that stage.

Soon after, one of the new carers was promoted to manageress. She seemed to be approachable and caring, and had an outgoing personality. We hoped with someone on board to oversee things, the situation at the home would improve and it would become more settled and better organised. Sadly, that was not the case.

One of our ongoing frustrations was the laundry system. The care home generated a great deal of washing on a daily basis, and this was done by the carers at the home. It was a common sight to see bed linen and other items draped over the bannisters to air or dry. Everything was washed at a very hot temperature so items were often shrunk or came out grey, or very stiff. Nothing was ever ironed, which we appreciate would have been a huge task, but garments were often horribly creased, as if they had been left in the washing machine or drier for too long. These items were not something you wanted to dress an elderly loved one in.

We frequently had to purchase new clothes for Mum as, although her garments were clearly marked, they still used to go astray. We would often find Mum wearing somebody else's clothes, but took exception when it was someone else's knickers, particularly, as did happen, when they were several sizes too small for her!

As a result, we decided to do Mum's washing ourselves, at home, and provided a laundry basket for carers' use. The exception was soiled items which, for obvious reasons, were to be immediately dealt with by the care home. All too often, though, we would find badly soiled underwear thrown in with her washing, making Mum's room smell very unpleasant, and ruining other clothes that might be mixed in with them. On one occasion, we found actual excrement in the laundry.

Often Mum's bed was poorly made with ill-fitting sheets and lumpy pillows. On one occasion, she had just a flat cushion on which to rest her head. We requested more pillows and these would appear for a day or so, only to disappear again. In truth, the narrow bed was seldom properly made and never looked particularly comfy.

We wrote to the manager, expressing our concerns about ongoing issues within the care home. For some reason, the manager didn't reply to this letter until July, some two months later. In her response she assured us that things were in hand and being dealt with.

Then there was a worrying visit by family members over the May bank holiday weekend. It was extremely hot and the commode in Mum's bedroom had not been emptied. The room smelt really bad and the window was shut. We assumed the commode must have been left since that morning as we visited in the afternoon and Mum was sitting downstairs, having finished her lunch.

None of the residents in the lounge with Mum had drinks when we arrived and were complaining of being hot and thirsty, so we asked the carers, who were chatting in the garden, if they could organise a jug of juice. Despite asking more than once, this didn't happen and we made tea for Mum and some of the other residents, although we weren't really supposed to do this for anyone other than Mum. Mum was dressed in someone else's clothes and her bed had a sheet on it that didn't fit properly, so it didn't reach the corners.

The following day, when visiting the care home, we found two residents in the lounge shouting for attention, while carers were again sitting in the garden chatting and smoking cigarettes. Mum also complained that carers had been rough with her and had hurt her. We reassured her and politely reminded the young carers on duty to be careful when handing her.

Mum was also without her alarm, to alert carers if she required assistance. In fact, this was a frequent occurrence. The smaller lounge where she sat during the day with Dot and Bob was a pleasant room. However, as carers were frequently busy in other parts of the home, the residents in the small lounge were frequently left unsupervised. The room also contained dangerous wobbly tables that sometimes would just collapse, causing us concern about them being used for hot drinks and meals. Rather alarmingly, residents would also lean on them to assist with getting up. We brought this hazard to the manager's attention but nothing was done about it at that time.

The following weekend, one of Mum's grandsons went to visit his nan with his wife and children. They had trouble gaining entry as no one came to answer the door in spite of them repeatedly knocking and ringing the bell. They also tried to attract someone's attention by calling through the back gates and they eventually gained access through the back garden.

Once inside, they found Mum in a distressed state as she desperately needed the toilet. Another resident said she also needed to go but no one had come to help her. They immediately looked for a member of staff, saying they were visiting Jean, and the two carers on duty came to help but only attended to Mum. They felt the carers had only come to help because they were visiting and had asked them directly.

The other lady was upset as she said she had asked first but was told she had to wait. Shortly afterwards, there was a strong smell of urine, suggesting she had had an accident. Again, they had to look for the carers, who they found chatting, and finally went to this lady's aid. Mum became very upset at the end of the visit and they were concerned to leave her.

The next day the manager rang to say she didn't think the home could continue to care for Mum as our expectations were too high! (Later, when we took our grievances to the Local Government and Social Care LGO, we discovered that The Owner had dismissed some of our concerns as 'nit-picking'.)

That same evening, Mum had a fall. We received a phone call from the young, inexperienced carer on duty. She said Mum had tried to get up to go to the toilet (using one of the unstable tables for support as her walking frame was not nearby) and had fallen. The carer asked if we could speak to the paramedics attending to run through Mum's medical history as she was unable to access her records and the senior carer on duty wasn't around, which we thought odd.

Immediately after receiving the call, Sue and Brian went to the care home to be with Mum. It was, by this time, around an hour or more after Mum had fallen. They found her upstairs in her room sitting in a wheelchair, attended by the paramedics, complaining of severe pain in her chest. She was extremely distressed, crying and begging for someone to take the pain away. The paramedics required assistance from the carers as Mum's blood pressure needed to be taken in a standing position. They had tried to alert a carer to help them using the call button in her room, but the button didn't work! The paramedics had been left alone to deal with Mum, so Sue went downstairs to locate a carer.

She found the senior carer on duty, who had not been in evidence previously, and the young carer we had spoken to on the phone, and they came up to help. The paramedics felt the pain was due to the fall and it would be better for Mum to get into bed. However, they were concerned she might have a urinary tract infection as she smelt of strong urine (although a test later proved this not to be the case).

While this was happening, other residents required assistance but there didn't seem to be enough carers on duty to deal with them. Sue asked the senior carer if the manager and owner had been notified and, some time after, The Owner, who lived very close, arrived at the home along with the manager.

Mum was settled in bed by the time The Owner marched into Mum's room, ignoring the paramedics and without introducing herself. She showed no sign of compassion and appeared to be more concerned about the impact on herself if any injuries had been sustained, rather than our poor mum. The atmosphere was heavily charged and it appeared to those present that The Owner was trying to provoke an argument. Sue was clearly upset and concerned about our mother, but The Owner would later accuse her of having had a bad attitude on that evening, expressed through her body language, and blaming her distress on the earlier phone call with the manager, when the home said they could no longer care for Mum. The attending paramedics did not seem impressed with The Owner's behaviour. In fact, one of them asked if we had considered moving Mum to another home.

The following day, we received another phone call from Care Home 1, requesting that we collect a letter from The Owner. We thought she might have had second thoughts about the way she had acted on the previous night and written an apology. This was not the case. In the letter, The Owner made inappropriate, unfounded accusations about Sue's behaviour. No compassion was shown about how distressing it must have been for Mum and us, nor was there any acknowledgement of the poor way the situation had been handled by the home. In fact, she went on to accuse the family of lack of respect when approaching carers. The letter appeared to have been hastily put together and was poorly written, with parts of it not making much sense. Not only was it unprofessional, the comments were untrue and hurtful.

The next day when we visited, we found Mum in bed. Her room was very smelly due to the commode again not having been emptied. She was still without an alarm button and had no way of alerting carers if she needed help. We were concerned about how Mum looked and requested she be seen by a doctor. Fortunately, there was no physical damage and she recovered from the shock of the fall, although our trust in the home had been further eroded.

Later, we wrote a response to The Owner's letter, expressing our deep regret that communication between ourselves and the management team had broken down and hoped this could, perhaps, be remedied by a meeting. At this point, we believed it was still in Mum's best interests to work with the management of the home. We were worried that a move might exacerbate the effects of Alzheimer's disease and cause Mum unnecessary stress and confusion.

Before the meeting was arranged, The Owner rang us at home late one evening. She suggested the reason we were questioning Mum's care was due to the influence of 'certain other families' at the care home, who had a 'negative attitude' and were colouring our view. She suggested that we should talk to 'more positive' relatives. We often spoke to a family member of another resident who had ongoing concerns about the care her dad was receiving and assumed this was to whom she was referring as being 'negative', but it seemed like a bizarre thing for someone in her position to say to a resident's family.

In August, a meeting was held between the manager and ourselves. A carer whom we had never met before was also present, and was introduced as the deputy manager. This was news to us, and further evidenced how little we were kept informed about the comings and goings of staff at the home. As communication with the home had become increasingly difficult, we requested that someone from Social Services also attend the meeting to mediate, but they weren't available.

During a full and frank conversation, many issues were discussed, but the manager was largely unable to comment in respect of events on the evening of Mum's fall as she had been absent for the majority of the time. We stressed that our primary concern was the welfare of our mother. We reiterated that we had the utmost respect for carers and staff and understood they had a difficult and important job to do. In fact, over the years, some of the carers who attended Mum had come to feel more like friends, although by this time, these had long since left the home's employ. We were told not to assist other residents, in future, but to alert carers on duty if someone required help. This was always our first call, and we had done so in the past, but this did not always result in action. Many questions about the circumstances of the night of the fall and The Owner's strange letter remained unanswered.

Then, on leaving the meeting, we bumped into The Owner who grudgingly agreed to have a brief chat with us, specifically to discuss the events of the 19th of July and her subsequent letter. Unfortunately, it appeared to us that attack was always The Owner's first response and she repeatedly talked over us, but we persevered in putting our point of view across. Eventually, she gave an apology for her previous comments, which did not feel sincere, and a fresh start was agreed. She then asked us to shred all correspondence we had received from her. Again, we felt this was an odd way for a professional care home provider to behave. Needless to say, we kept her letters, something we would be very glad about later.

Dos and Don'ts

Do:

- Try to resolve issues with the care provider in the first instance. Keep a record of meetings and telephone calls and make a note of what was said and the date. Make a copy of all correspondence. This may be useful later if you need to refer back to something, or escalate matters.
- Question the care your loved one is receiving if you think something is wrong, even if this feels difficult. Concerns about a care home, home-care agency or other adult social care service, should be reported to the local council in the first instance. Concerns about any care service can also be reported to the CQC to alert them of potential problems at a particular establishment.

Don't:

- Give up, even if, at first, you think no one is listening. Your priority is the care and safety of your loved one.
- Struggle alone. Seek advice from an appropriate agency if you need help (see the Useful Contacts section at the back of this book).

Facts and Figures

- When someone is asked to leave their care home, the home must clearly explain the reason why, and they must have a valid reason. For example, the care home can no longer meet their needs, or they have repeatedly failed to pay resulting in large arrears (Gov.uk/care-homes-consumer-rights-for-residents-and-their-families).

Chapter 8
Weddings and Births

In 1968, Sue married Brian. Kim was just five at the time and was a bridesmaid at the wedding, along with two of Sue's friends. Being the sixties, the older bridesmaids had beehive hairstyles pinned with flowers and Sue looked radiant in her fashionable wedding dress.

A local hall was hired and decorated for the reception. Mum and Dad, Peggy and Norman (Brian's parents) and friends came together to sweep and scrub the hall from top to bottom. Decorations were put up, barrels of beer were ordered and a catering company brought in to prepare the food. A local man was hired to act as DJ for the evening disco. A big bell filled with confetti hung over the top table ready to empty over the bride and groom when the wedding cake was cut. Naturally, we were joined by our extended family from the Midlands who were happy to be a part of the joyous celebrations. It turned out be a grand occasion.

Three years after the wedding, the first of five grandchildren arrived when Sue gave birth to Nicholas (Nick). Being the first grandchild, on both sides, he was naturally adored by all the family. Happy to be an aunty at such a young age, Kim fussed over her baby nephew. Mum loved to spend time with Sue and the baby, walking out with the pram and visiting local parks. Often, she would catch the bus at weekends spending the day at Sue and Brian's home. She was never happier than the time she spent with her grandson.

A couple of years later, grandchild number two arrived, who was named Gareth. So now Mum was a proud nan to two grandsons, and nothing gave her more pleasure than to be with them. Sue and Brian had, by then, moved nearer to Mum and Dad, and being closer gave Mum more precious hours to spend with her family. As soon as Kim got out of school, she would often go round as well to help keep the boys entertained.

There were always things to do; sunny days spent having picnics at the local beach, sandcastles to be built, shells to be collected and holes to be dug, as well as trips to the local park. As the boys grew there were birthday parties to organise and school functions to attend. Nothing ever seemed to faze Mum; she would always be there to lend a helping hand. With Mum being a keen knitter, the boys had plenty of baby clothes and warm jumpers.

The years rolled by and Kim moved to London, where she met her future husband, Mark, but she would still return home regularly to see her family. She later moved to Manchester to study for a degree in English and History. Mum and Dad were so proud when they attended the graduation ceremony, an event only slightly eclipsed by a visit to the nearby studios of *Coronation Street*, where they walked down those famous cobbles and enjoyed a pint in the Rover's Return.

Kim and Mark were married in 1992 and organised a day of celebration for family and friends. Once again, Mum helped to arrange everything, co-ordinating wedding gifts and helping to organise the reception at a nearby venue. The wedding took place in the same church where Sue and Brian had exchanged vows several years before and it was another wonderful, happy day.

Two years later, in 1994, Kim gave birth to Mum's eldest granddaughter, Emily Jean (after Emily Bronte, Kim's favourite author, and her two maternal grandmothers). At that time, Kim and Mark were living in South London. Mum, by then in her seventies, would make the two-and-a-half-hour journey by train, there and back, once a week, to spend the day with her daughter and Emily. Many happy hours were spent in Tooting Bec and Streatham Common. In 1997, Chloe arrived, much to everyone's joy, and Mum was kept busier than ever with two little girls to run around after.

When Emily reached school age, Kim and Mark moved back to our home town. Sue's boys were, by now, grown up and Gareth was, himself, father to two small boys; Lewis and Harrison (Harry). We would meet often, particularly in the summer months, and take the four children out for the day – with Mum, of course. We have many fond memories, and more than one or two funny stories from this time.

Two more children were to be born into the family, a daughter, Bryony, to Gareth and a son, Samuel (Sam), to Kim and Mark. This was a very happy time for Mum, surrounded by grandchildren and great-grandchildren, finally being able to enjoy the large family she always longed for.

There were now six young children to watch over on days out, and things did not always go to plan. On one memorable occasion at the beach, the older ones decided to walk across the mudflats, a fun thing to do when the tide was out. However, they did not turn back as usual and, instead, decided to keep heading out towards the sea.

As soon as we realised, we left Mum on the beach with the youngest and set off after the five children who, by now, had broken into a run. It was a windy day and our cries of 'stop' went unheeded. A little panicked, we increased our speed. The tide, when it turns, comes in very quickly and there are dangerous currents. Over the years, many people have found themselves in difficulty due to being cut off by the incoming tide. It's true that fear can lend you strength you didn't know you had and after an adrenaline-fuelled surge, we managed to catch up with the escapees, one by one. It gave us quite a fright, but we were too relieved to be cross for long.

A few years later, to everyone's delight, the family welcomed another great-grandson, George, to parents

Nicholas and Tricia. Mum was especially elated at having another baby to fuss over. This was quickly followed by the births of Joshua and Bethany. Unfortunately, this was just before Mum's health started to deteriorate, although she was still able to get a great deal of pleasure from family occasions for some time to come and many new memories were made with the arrival of each generation.

Chapter 9
Eviction!

The situation at Care Home 1 did not improve, in fact, it quickly became much worse. Mum had begun to lose weight and this seemed to accelerate, becoming a big concern.

Because she had become so frail, Mum was now routinely hoisted, something she found extremely upsetting. The hoist felt like an instrument of torture, often marking her skin where it was fragile and would tear and bruise easily. Some carers appeared to be insensitive to this fact, ignoring Mum's pleas and cries. Sadly, at times, it felt to us like this was just another chore to be done at speed, almost ignoring that she was there. Mum found the experience humiliating and distressing and it was horrible for us to watch. (This did not apply to all carers, and many tried their best but were too rushed to take time and adequate care.)

Other things had deteriorated generally around the care home. Again, there was a rapid turnover and noticeable shortage of staff. Around this time, the manager decided to move Mum into the larger of the two lounges, without prior discussion with ourselves. She said this was so carers could keep a closer eye on her. Fair enough, but Mum was confused about where she was as the surroundings were unfamiliar. She was also sitting next to residents she didn't recognise and was no longer with Dot and Bob. They may have believed this was in her best interests, but it didn't seem this way to Mum; it felt more like a punishment.

In early September, we made an appointment with the doctor responsible for residents (Mum had to leave the care of her GP whom she had been with for many years when she moved to Care Home 1) to express our concern at the rapid deterioration in her health. We discussed the continuing weight loss and the general decline in her health. The doctor was not particularly helpful or interested and suggested that Mum had lived a long life and problems were to be expected. He even told us she was well past her allotted 'three score years and ten'! We swallowed down a rude retort and asked what more could be done to help Mum. He said she should be encouraged and assisted to eat, and high calorie nutritional shakes should be increased to twice daily. We passed this information on to the home and were assured that this was in hand.

However, in the days that followed, we would often find plates of untouched food in front of Mum. Sometimes the food was unsuitable; either too difficult for her to chew or too spicy (Mum never liked spicy food, something the home was aware of). On one occasion, the young, inexperienced carer on duty served spicy wedges with oven chips as a meal! The shakes were prepared for Mum but, frequently, we found them untouched on the table, congealed and unappetising. So, as much as possible, one of us would try to be there at meal times. Sometimes, we would prepare and take in food we knew she liked, and sit and feed her.

This was a difficult time for us as we tried to ensure someone was always available to check in on Mum and encourage her to eat, while continuing with our daily lives. We had, by this point, lost trust in the care home and all those supposed to be looking after her. This was not how it was meant to be and far from what we imagined when we had taken the difficult decision for Mum to move into a care home.

Other things also started to be a concern. Mum frequently looked unkempt, wearing dirty clothes, with tangled, matted hair, as if it hadn't been brushed. The latter was particularly sad for us as one of the things Mum loved was for us to brush her hair (Mum maintained a full and thick head of hair throughout her life), something we had routinely started to do during our visits as she enjoyed it so much. It was difficult for her to have her hair washed as often in the care home, although there was a visiting hairdresser who used to do the ladies' hair (how beautiful they all looked on those days), but Mum would always sigh in pleasure whenever we brushed her hair. We felt these simple things were important to her continued well-being.

Then there was her false teeth. Mum always hated the dentist and, unfortunately, this had led to her having dentures. Quite often they would go missing, only to turn up in the most unlikely places. Mum had a habit of taking them out, wrapping the plate in tissue and putting it in her pocket and, on one occasion, they went through the washing machine with the top she had been wearing! Another time, we couldn't work out what was wrong with Mum's face. Why did she look so different? It transpired that she was wearing someone else's false teeth instead of her own.

It was not uncommon for Mum to have sticky hands and dirty fingernails, as if she had been out digging in the garden. She had inexplicably started to suffer from bad bouts of diarrhoea, and sometimes we witnessed it running down her trouser leg. It wasn't until later we realised the dirty fingernails were sometimes due to Mum relieving the itch caused by her own mess. When we queried the cause of her frequently upset tummy with the carers, it was dismissed as her becoming doubly incontinent due to old age and Alzheimer's disease, and was to be expected. We were well aware of some of the possible unpleasant developments of the later stages of Alzheimer's, but this did not quite seem true to us.

In early October, we were contacted by Social Services who arranged to see us, as a follow up to the meeting we had with the manager back in July. We met with a young social worker whom we had never met, who didn't know us or Mum and seemed very inexperienced. We explained to her how bad things had become and our ongoing concerns about the home and the care Mum was receiving. For whatever reason, we knew things weren't right. Social Services said they would visit the home, and we made it clear communication was strained and the situation needed to be handled carefully. We didn't want Social Services to damage our already fragile relationship with the management. Mum was by now ninety-three years old and in poor health. We told the social worker that we didn't feel it would be fair to put Mum through any additional trauma, and did not think she would survive a move.

On the afternoon of that same day, Sue went to visit Mum. Social Services had just left, having been in to see Mum and speak to the manager. As a consequence, Sue was called into the care home office. She was then told it had been decided by the home that it would be in the best interests of the family to look for an alternative home for Mum. Sue tried to question her about this and requested a meeting so that this could be discussed fully with Kim and other members of the family. This was declined, and no other discussion took place as the manager was in a hurry to leave to pick up her children from school. That evening, the enormity of this news and the potential consequences for Mum weighed heavily on us all.

The next day was Saturday. We went to visit Mum as normal, hoping that things might still be resolved amicably. As it was a weekend there was no manager on duty and only the usual skeleton staff, so there was no chance of further discussion. We were very alarmed by how dangerously frail Mum was now looking. To us, the situation seemed critical, but none of the carers seemed to be concerned. We felt anxious and alone.

On Monday afternoon, the manager rang Sue to ask how the family were getting on with finding a home for Mum. Her attitude was very casual, as if this were a normal conversation to be having with the family of a very elderly, obviously very unwell resident. At this point, no official letter or explanation had been received. When we asked the reason for this decision, she said the reasons had already been made clear. We then rang The Owner, who declined to discuss further, stating we had thirty-one days to find a new home and, at the end of that period, Mum would have to leave. We would deal with the full, unfolding horror of the situation at a later date. Our immediate concern was in finding a suitable new home for Mum.

By now, we trusted neither Social Services, nor the management of Care Home 1. We felt very much on our own. There was no support system in place and it felt like there was nowhere to turn for help. However, we had little time to consider the consequences or question the legality of such a decision. There was no time to think or plan, we had to act and fast.

The next day we visited several care homes in the area, revisiting some that we had looked at previously and had liked, narrowing down our search. In light of the urgency of our situation, Mum's poor health and the fact that our first experience with residential care had ended badly, it was a daunting prospect.

One home in particular had a vacancy, and the manager made us feel very welcome. We had previously expressed an interest and been on their waiting list, following a visit when we were initially looking for somewhere for Mum. It was a large detached house in a quiet, residential area with a big garden and visitors' parking at the front. More importantly, the home had a lovely warm feeling and all the residents looked clean and happy. It was noticeable that there were several staff on duty, all busy, and how efficiently it was run.

The only thing we were less certain about was that Mum would be sharing a bedroom with one other lady. As she was used to having her own room, we weren't sure how she would feel about this. However, it was the only room available at that time. (As it happened, Mum enjoyed the company, and she would continue to share a room, with three different ladies – all of them lovely – throughout her time living in the care home.)

Happily, Zara, the manager of the care home made us an offer to accept Mum, and they could take her in almost immediately. We were, and still are, very grateful.

At one of the other care homes we visited, we chatted with a lovely carer who sometimes worked at Care Home 1. She said she was very sorry to hear about Mum. We thanked her and asked how she knew Mum was leaving. The carer told us she had been made aware we had been told to move Mum during the previous weekend, while working at Care Home 1. The carers had been talking about it. This was before the

Termination of Occupancy letter had been issued and we had officially been informed. This felt wrong to us. In fact, we did not receive the official termination notice until the following Tuesday. And, still, no explanation was forthcoming. We came to our own conclusion; that Mum was being made to leave her home because we had questioned the care she was receiving.

While we were out visiting care homes, we stopped for lunch at the café attached to a local venue. In the foyer, we got talking to a lady who, coincidentally, was there campaigning about dementia on behalf of the NHS. We spoke about our experiences going through the care system with Mum, and her recent eviction - for that was how we saw it although this terminology was strongly refuted by The Owner. She enquired which home Mum was in. When we told her she said that she had had a relative living there, and her family had moved her. One of the things they complained to the home about was how unkempt she looked, and she always had dirt underneath her fingernails!

The following weekend, Sue arrived at Care Home 1 at 12.20 pm, in plenty of time to help Mum with her dinner. She found Mum slumped in her chair and it was difficult to rouse her. A nutritional shake had been left on her table; a skin had formed over the top of it which made it look most unappetising. When Mum woke up she asked for her usual cup of tea, so Sue removed the shake to throw away. However, she was intercepted by the woman we now knew to be the deputy manager, who pointed to the untouched shake like a formidable school mistress and said it was full of vitamins and Mum should try to drink it. So it was given a stir to encourage Mum to try it. On reflection, we couldn't help wondering how long it had been left there as, in a previous discussion, the deputy manager had stated she wouldn't give residents shakes just before meal times so as not to put them off eating.

The dinner served was a rather heavy-looking lasagne, spiced wedges (of course!) and vegetables. Not really a suitable dinner for an elderly resident who needed encouragement to eat. Another resident was served mash and mince so Sue asked if Mum could possibly have the same. The deputy manager grudgingly brought a portion in a small dish.

While still trying to coax Mum to drink the shake, unfortunately, it spilled down her trousers and she had to be changed. Sue accompanied Mum and returned to find the mince had been thrown away as the deputy manager thought it had been hanging around for too long. Weird, as the shake had obviously been sitting there for much longer!

Mum was sleepy so Sue chatted to the family of another resident, something we would often do, who inquired how Mum was. Sue told them that Mum was being forced to leave the home and would be moving the following Tuesday. They were understandably shocked. Sue explained that there had been a lot of issues since Mum had a fall in July but the follow up with Social Services had resulted in a Termination of

Occupancy letter being issued. Sue also had a brief conversation with the daughter of the lovely man who now sat next to Mum, explaining what had happened. Nothing defamatory was said against the home or management, in fact, at that time, we attributed Social Services' poor handling of the situation for Mum being made to leave.

At this point, Stuart walked in for a visit, although he was no longer employed by the home. He was, by now, well-known to Mum and our family, and had always been good to us, and he came over to say how sorry he was that Mum was leaving. Sue asked if he knew the whereabouts of Mum's wheelchair, as it seemed to have gone missing, but he couldn't recall what had happened to it. This was the full extent of the conversation which later seemed to annoy The Owner who said we shouldn't have been talking to him.

About hour or so later, Mum woke up feeling hungry and Sue asked it was possible to get her something to eat. The deputy manager said it was too near tea time she would have to wait. So much for encouraging her to eat! Sue then sat silently with Mum, who refused to let go of her hand.

At around 3.00 pm that same afternoon, The Owner arrived and had a short conversation with the deputy manager. She then proceeded to shout at Sue from across the other side of the lounge, in front of Mum and the other residents, before ordering her to leave the premises, saying if she refused to go, she would call the police. At the time, we had no idea why. It later transpired it was because The Owner alleged that Sue had spoken to other residents' families about Mum being forced to leave, and to Stuart. The Owner did not give Sue a chance to explain, or even speak. Instead, as usual, she continued to talk over her.

Sue's grandson, Lewis, and his wife, Laura, then arrived to visit their great nan with the intention of giving Sue a lift home afterwards. They found their nan (Sue) in tears, and politely suggested that they all go into the office to talk in private. The Owner then suggested that this was a racial issue. The family were taken aback by this, as all we ever wanted was to ensure Mum's care and well-being was up to the required standard. The ethnicity of The Owner, or anyone else for that matter, had never been in any way relevant.

By this time, Mum had become so distressed that Lewis and Laura went over to console her while an extremely upset Sue went to collect Mum's laundry. When Sue returned, she was told by Lewis that The Owner had gone over to them, in front of Mum who they had been trying to comfort, and ordered them to remove Sue from the premises. As far as they were aware, there were no other residents' families present at that time, only the deputy manager and another carer on duty. On leaving, they encountered another resident's family returning from an outing, but no discussion took place.

Early the following morning (Sunday), The Owner rang Kim and told her that Sue was banned from Care

Home 1, and could no longer visit Mum, because of her 'disruptive behaviour'. She was extremely rude and aggressive and said Sue had upset other residents and their families. This was untrue. It was The Owner who had been shouting, and causing upset. The call was on speaker phone and Kim's husband, Mark, was listening in. They politely told The Owner never to call again.

With Sue forbidden to enter the home (we were later told this was a breach of Mum's human rights) Kim spent as much time as possible with Mum, trying to prepare her for the move. This was difficult, as she also needed to pack up Mum's things, as well as try to explain what was happening, but couldn't do both at the same time. Another family at the home said how sorry they were that Mum was leaving and expressed their disgust at how we had been treated. This was the family that had concerns about their loved one, who was still living there. They were afraid of speaking out and the consequences of upsetting The Owner. We were proof of what could happen if you did.

On the 16th of October Mum moved to Care Home 2. Sue was 'allowed' in the home to assist with last minute packing and to help with Mum. We had, again, asked Social Services if they would mediate, as we could foresee many problems. Inevitably, they declined to help.

We arranged a wheelchair taxi for 10.00 am and requested the manager to leave Mum in relative comfort in one of the lounge chairs and only transfer her to the wheelchair when the taxi arrived. We knew sitting for long periods in her wheelchair would cause her unnecessary suffering. When we arrived at the pre-arranged time of 9.00 am, we found Mum in the lounge, on her own, already hunched over in her wheelchair. She looked very uncomfortable and was extremely upset and in severe pain, with no understanding of what was happening. She looked a sad sight and it made us very angry. How could anyone treat a confused, distressed, old lady in poor health in this appalling way, let alone carers who had been charged with looking after her?

While Kim tried to comfort and reassure Mum, Sue and Brian hurried to clear the remaining things from her room. We had decided to take the chest of drawers provided by us to the new home, as they would be useful. While negotiating the stairs with the drawers, they came face to face with The Owner who accused us of stealing property that belonged to the home. When it had been confirmed that the drawers did, indeed, belong to us, The Owner told staff to check what we were taking, and we were shadowed the entire time.

In the run up to Mum leaving, many had expressed how sorry they were to see her go. The staff on duty were very quiet on the actual day, but one lovely carer hugged us all in tears and said she sincerely hoped Mum would be happy in her new home. At that moment, looking at her skeletal frame slumped in the unforgiving wheelchair, we just hoped she would survive the journey.

Dos and Don'ts

Do:

- Contact your local Social Services immediately if you or your loved one is served notice on their care home.
- Be open-minded and consider all options if you do have to make a move, even if they aren't part of your preferred plan (for example, in the past, we would not have considered a shared room for Mum, but it worked out well).

Don't:

- Be afraid to ask for the reason for a 'notice to quit' if none is forthcoming and to question this decision.

Facts and Figures

- If a care home stops a resident from receiving visitors, this may be a breach of the resident's right to have family life protected. Any action that breaches human rights must be legitimate and proportionate (Human Rights Act 1998).
- When a resident in a care home is issued a 'notice to quit', Section 5 of the Protection of Evictions Act 1977 (PEA) states that the home must provide at least twenty-eight days' notice in writing (source as above).

Chapter 10
Holidays and High Days

September 1983 was Mum and Dad's Ruby Wedding Anniversary. We decided to treat them to an overseas holiday in Sorrento, Italy. Dad used to talk a lot about Italy as he was stationed there during the war, so it was agreed that Sorrento was the best destination. Lots of planning and secrecy was required. We asked Joan and Frank if they would like to go along and they were delighted to accept the invitation.

We made a scrapbook of the past forty years, starting with Mum and Dad's wedding and finishing with some images and background information on Sorrento. We arranged to get together and give it to them during Christmas 1982, allowing plenty of time for holidays from work to be booked. They were very surprised and excited, especially when Sue found out that Brian had booked for them all to go, too.

Mum had never flown before, or indeed, been abroad and her joy as she looked forward to the holiday gave us great pleasure. As the year passed research was done to find out more about the area we were visiting. The time passed quickly and soon cases were packed, and arrangements had been made to meet Joan and Frank at Gatwick Airport as they were travelling from Bloxwich. Mum was so happy to be flying for the first time to a country she had always wanted to visit, with the family she loved.

We boarded the plane. Mum sat in a window seat, and Nicholas and Gareth took turns to hold her hand, as she gazed in awe at the sky outside. The plane headed south, flying over France and Switzerland to Italy, before landing at Naples airport. From there, the party boarded a coach, passing Mount Vesuvius before seeing Sorrento perched on top of the cliffs that separated the town from the busy marinas. It certainly didn't disappoint. The Amalfi coast was stunning, lined with grand villas overlooking the dramatic cliffs and picturesque coastline. In places the mountains seemed to plunge into the sea.

We tried to visit as many places as possible, taking Mum and the family to the Isle of Capri in the bay of Naples. After some persuasion, we managed to get everyone on a chair lift, which took us to the top of the island. We will always remember the look on Mum's face as she took in the breath-taking views, the lovely designer shops and the huge, luxurious yachts moored in the marina. Time was also spent on the beach, in the sea and sunbathing. It was a wonderful holiday, resulting in many happy memories which we talked about for years after.

Mum really enjoyed flying and this would not be her last flight in an aeroplane, although the next occasion would be very different. Her grandson Gareth works in aviation and one of his friends had recently learnt to fly light aircraft. Gareth asked if Mum would like to go up in a plane with him and his friend. Mum didn't hesitate and, one overcast Sunday afternoon, she was soaring above the clouds over Essex in a tiny plane with her grandson. Needless to say, she loved it. We were just glad we didn't find out about the flight, until after they had landed safely!

An annual highlight for many years was the local airshow, which took place above the Thames Estuary during the late May bank holiday. Mum loved everything about the airshow, which was always spectacular. So, the family would gather together, come rain or shine (and it has to be said that it was often wet or windy), to marvel at the display in the sky. Among our favourites over the years were the Red Arrows, the Battle of Britain Memorial Flight, the Tornado F3, Sea Vixen, Hawk T1, Vulcan, Typhoon, and the daring Breitling Wingwalkers. In earlier years, before Southend became a commercial airport, you could visit the airport and see some of the planes up close and mix with the crew, which was always a bit of a thrill. Sadly, the airshow was cancelled in 2013 due to austerity cutbacks by the council and was a great loss to the town and the community.

The end of the 20th century brought with it huge anticipation as the world looked towards the forthcoming Millennium. There was also much superstition and fear which, in hindsight, seems a bit silly. In 1999 there was apprehension that the so-called Y2K Millennium bug would cause global chaos. Many worried that when the clock struck midnight on the 1st of January, 2000, computers would fail due to problems in the coding of computerised systems. Until the 1990s many computer programs abbreviated the years to save memory space. So 1997 would be 97, but it was feared that it would not recognise 2000 as 00 causing widespread disruption. But in the end, of course, nothing happened and computers and technology continued to operate as we welcomed in the new century.

Being a special New Year, celebrations were organised across the world and we were no different. We planned a big gathering of family and friends for this momentous occasion. Naturally, Mum helped with the decorations and preparing the buffet. There were fireworks in the garden and a karaoke machine was set up on the television in the lounge. So there were lots of laughs, especially if one of us tone deaf sisters took the mic. As it happened, Mum turned out to be the Queen of the Karaoke, belting out favourite tunes. It was an evening full of fun and laughter, creating more happy memories.

Mum and Dad's wedding day; 19th September, 1943.

Some of the Morgan clan, Bloxwich. Our maternal grandma and grandad are centre row right. Sue is in the front row, second right.

Jean with her mum (our Grandma Morgan) and sister, Joan, on one of many trips to the Midlands.

Our family, circa 1967, Mum and Dad centre, with Sue at the back and a young Kim.

Mum with her daughters at a family wedding.

Dad and Mum during a visit to Coronation Street, Manchester during the 1980s.

Celebrating Mum and Dad's 50th wedding anniversary in Bloxwich, 1993, shortly before the singing began.

A growing family: grandchildren and great-grand children, 2003. Mum loved spending time with them.

Kim with her three children and their nan during one of many trips out for lunch.

Four generations, including Mum, Sue & Brian, their sons and their children.

Her favourite homemade Victoria sponge with jam and cream for Mum's birthday.

A family visit when Mum was living in residential care.

Chapter 11
Care Home 2

Mum moved into Care Home 2 in mid-October, 2018. Everyone made her and our family feel very welcome, and there was a busy, happy and positive atmosphere. However, the most striking thing to us was the efficient way it was run, under the sharp-eyed guidance of the manager, Zara. There were far greater numbers of staff visible on each shift than there had been at Care Home 1, many of whom had worked at the home for several years. The carers treated the residents like friends, and it felt like a cheerful, safe and settled environment.

When Mum arrived, nothing was too much trouble and she was quickly made clean and comfortable. The manager and staff were shocked at her unkempt state and dirty appearance and immediately gave her a bath, something they apparently wouldn't normally do until a resident was more settled. They, like us, were horrified to discover Mum weighed just five and a half stone.

Zara raised concerns about Mum's frail condition, bruising, possibly caused by poor handling, and the condition of her feet. Mum had a nasty, untreated sore under her toenail and it would take several weeks to heal, in spite of us having paid for Mum's feet to be taken care of by a chiropodist at Care Home 1. The chiropodist at Care Home 2 was astonished that Mum's feet had been allowed to get in such a state.

Zara also arranged for a full review of medication when it was discovered that Mum had been prescribed, and appeared to have been taking, several different laxatives. It was difficult to prove that the laxatives were the cause of the diarrhoea that had plagued Mum's final weeks at Care Home 1, but as soon as they were stopped the diarrhoea and persistent upset stomachs did too. Mum immediately regained her appetite and, in those early days, ate everything she was given and asked for more. The care home staff would make her delicious sandwiches, at all hours of the day, and the food was always nutritious and appetising.

The staff seemed to be fond of Mum and were happy to make her the endless cups of tea she enjoyed throughout the day. "Tea for Jean," she would call out. Minutes later a cup of hot tea would appear in front of her. It wasn't long before Mum started to put on a little weight but we still had to buy her an entire new wardrobe of clothes. She had lost so much weight that her old clothes hung off her skeletal frame. We felt so guilty that she had got into this state, and blamed ourselves for allowing things to get so bad. We hadn't realised that moving her would be the best option, until our hand was forced.

At first, Mum was able to walk to the toilet, with the aid of her frame, but she was so frail by this point that she struggled to support her weight and, inevitably, she had to be hoisted. She still hated the hoist (and who can blame her?), but the staff were always gentle with her and she eventually became more used to it. To us, the hoist always seemed like a very undignified and uncomfortable contraption but we appreciated that staff had to protect their own backs and health. However, in our opinion, had Mum been encouraged to continue walking during her time at Care Home 1 and not been allowed to deteriorate into such a frail state, the hoist could have been avoided for much longer.

Although we experienced much sadness and many traumatic moments during Mum's care home life, there have also been good times to reflect on and some happy memories. Not long after Mum arrived at Care Home 2, they organised their annual Halloween party for residents, friends and families. The carers decorated the home, with a little help from the residents. Witches' hats and broomsticks, spiders and cobwebs were hung from the ceiling and walls. There was spooky-themed food and drink. This, of course, was a great opportunity for everyone to dress up, including Mum's three youngest great-grandchildren: George, Joshua and Bethany. They arrived at the care home, dressed up in scary costumes with painted faces – as did we! The carers made a huge effort and were also dressed up. We're not sure Mum fully appreciated the concept of so many weird faces surrounding her but nevertheless enjoyed having her family around her and watching as they took part in the fun and games.

There was also a summer fayre, with food and music and a lovely relaxed atmosphere. A relative of one of the carers also bought in some young rabbits, and residents and visitors enjoyed a cuddle with one or two of them. In fact, some of the rabbits needed a good home, and Jean's granddaughter, Emily, bought two fluffy bunnies. These 'females' then had a litter and two became six! Mum loved to see photos and video clips as the kittens grew from sleepy, furless newborns into lively (and extremely cute!) balls of energy, lolloping around the garden.

Quite often, a lady would take her dogs into the home. These were well-trained, gentle animals, used to being around people, who loved to be made a fuss of and petted. They were very popular with the residents.

Although Mum was now settled, the traumatic end to her time at Care Home 1 lingered. We felt that Mum had been unfairly punished because we had raised concerns about her welfare and wanted to prevent this from happening to anyone else. Unsure how to do this, we posted a review on a couple of care home sites, by way of a caution, explaining that the owner of Care Home 1 had forced a frail, elderly resident in poor health, to leave her home.

This included a review on Facebook, saying we could not recommend Care Home 1 as they had effectively evicted our ninety-three-year-old mother. The review was brief and stuck to the facts without being offensive, as it was meant to warn others, rather than attribute blame. However, what followed was an unprofessional outpouring of abuse and untruths on social media from the owner and manager of Care Home 1. Once again, The Owner suggested this was a race issue. All she had to do was say 'sorry', rather than turn it into a personal attack, but the vicious tirade against our family only reinforced what we had previously witnessed about her attitude. The post was swiftly taken down, but not before we had taken a screenshot of her hateful comments.

We subsequently discovered, through another review posted elsewhere online, that this was not the first time the owner of Care Home 1 had made a resident leave their home. The reviewer, dating back to 2015, stated that her father was asked to leave because he was 'fiddling with things' and breaking them as he suffered from dementia. The review suggested that the care home was not geared up to cope with residents with more complex needs, a view we shared, and moving someone suffering from dementia was 'detrimental to their health'. How could it not be?

It had been a relief when Mum moved as the situation had become unpleasant and unworkable at Care home 1. It is our belief that she wouldn't have survived much longer had she remained there. Our only regret was that we did not move her sooner but we felt that it would be too traumatic and confusing for her. Her health was deteriorating and we didn't want to cause additional distress. Not for the first time, we underestimated just how strong our Mum was.

We felt that Mum was in safe hands at Care Home

2 and we no longer felt anxious when we left after a visit. She responded well to their care and attention. As expected, she did get confused about where she was at times and we would often have curious conversations:

'I'm so relieved to see you. I was worried about how I would get home.'

'You are home, Mum, remember. This is where you live now.'

'Here? Oh that's very good of them. Are you sure they don't mind having me?'

'No, it's fine. It's all arranged.'

'Can you pay them for me? I think there's some money in my purse.' (Mum was always worried that she owed people money and loved to treat everyone.)

'There's no need, it's all settled.'

'Can my friends stay too?' (Meaning some of the other residents with whom she had become friendly.)

'Yes, of course. You can all stay here together.'

'Well, how kind and who knew…'

'Knew what, Mum?'

'That the church did bed and breakfast. I only came in to sing a few hymns and see my friends; now we're all staying the night.'

Around this time, we bumped into the family of one of the residents at Care Home 1. They asked after Mum and said how glad they were to hear that she was doing well. They went on to say that they were extremely dissatisfied and concerned about the care their relative was receiving. Unfortunately, they were too afraid of repercussions to speak out and complain to the authorities. Sadly, this was something that was said to us many times when families were unhappy with the care of a loved one in a care situation.

With the immediate concerns about Mum's health and well-being removed, we felt ready to raise questions with our local council social service complaints department about why things had been allowed to go so badly wrong at Care Home 1. Early in October, we contacted the Complaints Officer at the council who, disappointingly, seemed reluctant to investigate the Termination of Occupancy. On leaving Care Home 1, we had written a letter to The Owner, detailing our version of events leading up to the Termination of Occupancy, to which we had received a jumbled, unsatisfactory reply containing many untruths. It also failed to address the question of why our mother had been forced to leave her home. We suspected it was nothing to do with Mum and was because we had asked too many questions about Mum's 'care'. The Complaints Officer seemed to think the fact we had received a response meant the matter was closed, but we felt things were far from resolved.

However, the Complaints Officer did feel that there were grounds to open a safeguarding enquiry in respect of the apparent overuse of laxatives and weight loss. She then went on to say that the council would be unable to investigate the Termination of Occupancy alongside the safeguarding issues, although we felt the two were intrinsically linked. We received an email from the Complaints Officer confirming our conversation and the proposed course of action.

We didn't hear anything for some time and felt that the council perhaps weren't taking our concerns seriously or were too busy to investigate. So, in November 2018, we approached the Local Government and Social Care Ombudsman (LGO). In order to proceed, the LGO requires the consent of the person being investigated. As we had POA for Mum, this was submitted so that we could act on her behalf. The LGO allocated us with a case number, but then we hit another setback. They could not begin to look into our case until the outcome of the safeguarding enquiry had been received.

In early December, we were invited to a meeting at the local council offices with a female social worker, Single Point of Access (SPA), who was a representative of the council. It was a two-hour meeting in which we detailed the circumstances leading up to the Termination of Occupancy letter from Care Home 1.

The social worker appeared to be sympathetic and agreed that there was a case to answer. She then photocopied all correspondence between ourselves and the home and accompanying evidence such as photographs. We were told there would, most likely, be a meeting with Social Services and a representative from the CQC, to which the owner of Care Home 1 would be invited. It would provide us with an opportunity to discuss our grievances and for all parties to have their say. We were in full agreement and left the meeting feeling hopeful.

The first Christmas Mum spent at Care Home 2 was a much happier one. The residents were encouraged to make decorations with the aid of carers and family and the home was prepared for the festive season and Christmas party. There was an artificial Christmas tree and chimney stack post box for cards, made by the carers and residents. The owners of the care home joined in with the party bringing along delicious treats they had prepared that were traditionally used to celebrate special occasions in their own culture.

We sang carols with the residents when a visiting choir from a local church came in. Mum's face lit up as she joined in enthusiastically. She may have lost memories of Christmases past but the familiar carols transported her back to another time and place. She knew the words to them all and amazed the carers with her strong singing voice. In fact, there is a great deal of research to support the fact that music and singing, in particular, can be beneficial to people living with dementia.

In 2018, actress Vicky McClure formed a choir of people living with dementia to see if music could make a difference to their quality of life, resulting in a moving two-part BBC series *Our Dementia Choir.* Influenced by personal experience of helping to care for her grandma, who suffered from dementia, Vicky had witnessed first-hand the amazing effect music can have in calming down dementia sufferers and providing a window back to the person they used to be. The Dementia Choir has continued to prove to be a great success, making a real difference to people suffering from dementia and raising funds and awareness of this cruel syndrome. Vicky is a strong campaigner for reform of the social care system.

We were obviously sad not to be able to take Mum home over Christmas but it would have been too difficult at this point. However, we both went in with presents at different times of the day, so she didn't spend too long without a visitor. By this point, Mum wasn't always certain of the day or year, but happily opened presents for her 'birthday'.

In the New Year, we followed up with the Complaints Officer in respect of the safeguarding investigation, and were told the council could find no evidence of wrongdoing. It was not clear if anyone from the council had visited Care Home 1, whether the visit was announced or unannounced and what records, if any, had been checked. It was frustrating and we didn't feel we were being listened to.

In mid-January 2019, we received a report from Mum's new doctor detailing all her medication since her arrival at Care Home 1. To us, it made shocking reading and we wondered why a more regular review did not appear to have been carried out. She was taking the maximum dose of paracetamol, in addition to morphine patches and appeared to have been prescribed four different types of laxatives. The paracetamol was stopped on her arrival at Care Home

2 and given only when required and the type and frequency of patches changed. It made a big difference to Mum to have her pain relief managed effectively and we felt she was more comfortable as she complained much less. The report showed the frequency that the various medicines had been requested, including prescriptions for the laxatives, which appeared to correspond to the period she started with severe diarrhoea, but we had no documentary proof of what had been administered as Care Home 1 did not provide any.

In mid-February, we had a further meeting with the allocated social worker (SPA), again at the local council offices. It was our impression that she seemed to agree with us that the safeguarding issues should have been looked into as part of a broader picture, including the fall Mum suffered at Care Home 1 the previous summer while in their care. We showed her the medication report, which was duly photocopied and added to the already bulging file. The social worker told us it would be reviewed by a medical professional. She also promised to discuss the case with the relevant Team Leader, at Social Services, whom we understood would be overseeing the case. We left the meeting feeling that she wanted to help us.

Then, on the 8th of March, much to our surprise, we received a poorly written letter from the aforementioned Team Leader. It was riddled with typing errors, as if dashed out in a hurry, and even Kim's surname was spelt incorrectly. In spite of the documentation we had previously supplied to the social worker (SPA) allocated to our case, the letter stated they could find no supporting evidence of mistreatment. It also contained incorrect information that, as far as we could tell, must have come from Care Home 1. The letter appeared to imply, although this was not actually stated, that someone from the council had visited Care Home 1 and found all records in relation to Mum to be in order. We have no way of knowing if a visit took place, or whether, as we suspected, the council simply spoke to the management of Care Home 1 and took their word for it. None of the council's suggestions of a meeting and full investigation had come to anything. It seemed to us as if the council just wanted us to go away quietly and stop bothering them. It was a serious blow, but there was no way we were giving up.

We responded in a two-page letter to the Team Leader on the 16th of March contesting their findings and expressing our disappointment that the council refused to investigate further. On a more positive note, we were now able to pursue matters with the LGO.

Dos and Don'ts

Do:

- Write a positive review if you have had a good experience with a care provider as this will help to inform others in their choice of home.

Don't:

- Be afraid to speak up if your experience has been less positive as this may warn others of possible issues and possibly help to bring about change.

Facts and Figures

- As at August, 2022, there were around 17,100 care homes in the UK. Roughly seventy per cent of care homes were residential settings, with nursing homes accounting for up to thirty per cent of the total number (carehome.co.uk).
- Around seventy per cent of residents in UK care homes have dementia or severe memory problems (Alzheimer's Society).

Chapter 12
Milestones and Celebrations

Mum and Dad's fiftieth wedding anniversary fell within a month of Sue and Brian's twenty-fifth and Kim and Mark's first. The occasion warranted a big celebration and we organised a surprise party for Mum and Dad.

Although she loved to dance and sing and always joined in enthusiastically at family celebrations, Mum had seldom, if ever, had a party of her own. Born into a large family, in pre-war Britain, there was never enough money for parties or even many presents. Mum always told us she was grateful to receive just one present, along with a tangerine and a coin in her Christmas stocking as a child.

In later years, Mum was always more involved in organising and hosting parties for her daughters and family members. The majority of the Morgan clan had descended on our home town for a big party for Kim's 18th birthday. Mum hired a hall, arranged for relatives to stay with family and friends and oversaw decorating the hall. On the day, she got up early to make sandwiches and stuff vol-au-vents (popular at that time). She worked tirelessly and it was down to her hard work and planning that it was such a great success. Mum was always on hand for other people's parties. We felt it was time she enjoyed one of her own.

We hired a hall and secretly invited family and friends. Food was prepared at home and stored in friends' and neighbours' fridges and freezers (for once Mum didn't have to make the sandwiches). On the day of the party, the family met at the venue to help decorate the walls with balloons, banners and photographs. We had bought Mum and Dad two comfy, reclining garden chairs and a table for their Golden Wedding anniversary present and these were arranged in the centre of the hall like thrones, and festooned with balloons. A bottle of Champagne and two flutes were on the table, ready for their arrival. All we had to do was get them there without them suspecting anything.

We told Mum and Dad we were taking them out for a quiet family meal to celebrate our respective anniversaries. Kim and Mark were still living in London at that time, and staying with Mum and Dad, so were charged with bringing them to the venue. Our parents were expecting a restaurant but said nothing as the car pulled up outside of the hall. When they entered the assembled guests shouted 'surprise'.

The look on Mum's face made all the hard work and subterfuge worthwhile. Mum and Dad were escorted to their 'thrones', the Champagne was opened and duly poured, and a large bouquet put into Mum's arms. They were completely stunned. How we managed to keep the secret, we will never know, but they had absolutely no idea. It was a fantastic, memorable evening and Mum enjoyed being the centre of attention for once.

The party had been arranged on the most convenient day for all the family and Mum and Dad's actual fiftieth wedding anniversary fell on a different weekend, so we drove them to the Midlands for a grand dinner with Mum's siblings and their partners. It was the first time in a long while that all the brothers and sisters had been together, and it was a very special occasion.

Afterwards we all piled into Joan and Frank's tiny front room where a huge cake was cut and more Champagne flowed. What followed was a very special memory. Everyone present joined in a sing-song, belting out all the family favourites in fine voice. It was a wonderful evening, and a glimpse into a time long past, when people generated their own entertainment and would gather together to sing. Sadly, it was also the last time the brothers and sisters would all be together.

Ten years later, in 2003, Mum and Dad would celebrate sixty years of marriage. Mum was very happy when she received a congratulatory card from the then Queen. Their sixtieth wedding anniversary was celebrated with a family get together. To commemorate the occasion, we hired a photographer to record the event and have some lovely family pictures to remember the day.

Sadly, Dad died two years later.

Chapter 13
Justice for Jean

In April 2019, we again contacted the LGO who carried out an initial assessment to decide if there appeared to be a case to answer. In May, we received an email stating the LGO was taking on our case and we would hear from them shortly. However, due to the large volume of complaints they were dealing with at that time, this didn't happen until the beginning of July when an investigator was allocated to our case. We were delighted that at last someone was going to listen to us, investigate our concerns about Care Home 1 and the reasons Mum had been made to leave. We privately dubbed our fight 'Justice for Jean'.

In the event of a dispute with a care home, the local council is supposed to mediate and look into any complaints. If they fail to do so, the case can then be referred to the LGO, so we had to make our case against the council for not resolving matters satisfactorily and it was, therefore, their responsibility to obtain evidence from the care home. Both parties, ourselves and the council, had a period of time to submit their case and supporting evidence. Rather bizarrely, we thought, the council contacted us directly, asking to see our application to the LGO.

Suddenly, they appeared to be interested in what we had to say. We declined, as we felt it was for the council to make their own case regarding their efforts to protect a vulnerable person in their care.

We prepared our case carefully and submitted twenty-eight pieces of evidence, including a timeline of events, copies of all correspondence between ourselves and the care home documenting our concerns, testimonies from family members about what they had witnessed on visits to Care Home 1, screenshots of the comments on social media, medical reports, MARs (Medication Administration Records) charts from Care Home 2 evidencing Mum's progress since the move, and the letter from the Team Leader at the council.

Our application also included a few photographs. From time to time, we had taken photographs to show to the manager of Care Home 1 when we raised a concern. These included soiled clothes left in the laundry basket in Mum's room. There was also a photo of Mum's bed, with ill-fitting bedclothes and a lumpy cushion for a pillow. Another photo showed her dirt-encrusted fingernails shortly before she left Care Home 1.

It took some time to collate everything but our evidence was presented on time. Again, due to the number of cases they were dealing with and the complexity of our case, it was towards the end of the year before The Investigator was in a position to begin reviewing the case.

Christmas 2019 was to be the last Christmas that we were able to see Mum, due to COVID-19, although we couldn't have foreseen this at the time. Mum's extended family all visited over the festive period with gifts, mince pies and homemade Christmas cake – Mum's recipe that she had passed down. We both visited on Christmas Day, again at different times, to ensure she wasn't without family for most of the day. It was the first time that Mum showed little interest in Christmas, although she enjoyed the lovely Christmas dinner cooked by the care home staff (we were so thankful to them for giving up their day to look after Mum and the other residents). Mum had a great many presents and we enjoyed opening them with her, a few at a time, during the course of the following week.

In January, 2020, we received the Draft Decision from the LGO. They had found in our favour on the majority of points. Both parties (ourselves and the council) were given time to review the report and provide feedback and, again, we did so in a timely manner.

We contested two items raised in the lengthy report. The first related to an allegation by the owner of Care Home 1 that we had rolled our eyes 'at a new resident due to her race'. We never gave any thought to someone's ethnicity, only the care Mum and other residents were receiving. She also said we had 'made comments about non-English speaking staff', which was an odd thing to say considering all of the staff spoke fluent English, and this really had nothing at all to do with our grievances about the quality of care provided.

The second point we contested was a statement by Care Home 1 that we had made 'repeated threats' to move Mum to another care home and she had become distressed by this. Again, this was untrue. We tried very hard throughout Mum's time at Care Home 1 to work with management and staff to resolve issues as we felt it would be too traumatic for Mum if we tried to move her. Any conversations we had about her well-being were always conducted well out of her hearing. As there was obviously no evidence to support either of these allegations, both clauses were subsequently removed from the Final Decision.

In mid-February, we had an email from The Investigator saying she had received information 'direct from the Care Provider' (Care Home 1) stating she had 'not previously received all the information and/or it was not organised effectively'. Care Home 1 said they did not agree with The Investigator's report and had 'sent information to challenge this'. The council was also invited to inspect the new evidence. We were frustrated at the delay but thanked The Investigator for being thorough and waited to hear the outcome.

Two clauses were disputed by Care Home 1. The first was overuse of laxatives. The LGO's report drew attention to Mum's care plan, which stated: 'staff to ensure bowels are charted' and that she should 'be reviewed by the incontinence team regularly'. The report said there was no evidence of such a review and few records of Mum's bowel movements, apart from an occasional mention in her daily notes. It was further stated 'some of the medication sheets were poorly completed, with dates overwritten and unclear'.

The second related to weight loss. The report said Mum's care plans 'indicated she was at risk of weight loss' but 'this was simply stated and not set out in the usual form of a risk assessment'. There appeared to be discrepancies and inconsistencies in record keeping with the daily notes saying one thing, and the food chart another. The records showed that Mum had lost 4kg in two months and the doctor had been contacted (at our request). However, the 'handwritten note of the GP's response, added to the note of the call' was largely illegible. It stated 'no further action but offer extra [nutritional supplement] shakes', but this was not in the record of GP/nurse visits and calls.

In March 2020 we received the Final Decision from the LGO which upheld our complaints that the council 'provided residential care' to Mum 'which was not adequate' and 'provided care which was terminated when [we] complained about the poor service'.

The report acknowledged that our concerns, raised with the manager and the owner of Care Home 1, over several months, had not been addressed and we were not just 'nit-picking' as suggested by Care Home 1. It stated that Mum and the council 'were paying for a service' and Mum 'was entitled to have care which did not fall below the standards required in any way'. It further said that our complaints were not 'an adequate reason to give notice'. The report stated that moving homes was likely to cause distress to Mum and was, therefore, 'a potential breach of regulations' set out in the Health and Social Care Act 2008 and would be shared with the CQC.

The report went on to say that the 'Care Provider did not make enough effort to resolve' our 'valid complaints and concerns' and this should not have affected Mum's placement. It also found fault with the council for taking 'the Care Provider's responses at face value' and not looking for the documentation which might have shown that care was inadequate. Additionally, it stated there was a further breach of regulations by Care Home 1 for poor record keeping and 'the council's failure to follow up the concerns effectively was also at fault', causing us 'significant time, trouble, stress and frustration'.

The LGO found in our favour on all but two points, the exception being overuse of laxatives and weight loss and these sections were removed from the Final Decision. Additional records, which were only discovered after the Draft Decision was received, absolved Care Home 1 of wrongdoing in this respect. We can only repeat here that as soon as the laxatives were stopped, so did the diarrhoea.

The LGO's report contained a long list of recommendations. The council was asked to apologise to ourselves and Mum, 'setting out the faults' listed in the report and the action it would take to address them, and arrange for 'a similar apology from the Care Provider'. They were also asked to reimburse a small percentage of the fees paid by Mum and awarded us each a small sum in compensation (which we donated to the Alzheimer's Society). The council was also asked to review the service provided at Care Home 1 to ensure it met the required standards in respect of our concerns.

In addition, the council was tasked with raising awareness in staff who deal with complaints that 'they understand where it might not be appropriate to rely on a Care Provider's account in response to a complaint'. They were given three months to implement these actions and provide evidence to the LGO that they had been carried out. The council was subsequently granted additional time to put these measures in place because, by this time, COVID-19 had arrived and they had to address the escalating situation in care homes and other areas.

Ultimately, we had mixed feelings about the outcome. The process took months and was emotionally draining, but our grievances had finally been properly investigated. It was a relief that someone had listened to our concerns and the council and care home were to be made accountable for their actions. However, we felt that Mum was not adequately compensated for the distress caused. Of course, we have no way of knowing what effect the LGO report ultimately had on the way things are run at Care Home 1 and at our local Social Services Department (although

Care Home 1 was downgraded in a subsequent inspection by the CQC, stating that improvement is required in the areas of management and safety). We can only hope our actions brought about positive change and spared other families from the stress and worry we endured.

As previously mentioned, during the time Mum was in care, we spoke to many other families who also had concerns about loved ones living in care homes, but were too afraid to speak up for fear of retribution. We hoped that by speaking up, it might also help others in a similar situation to find the courage to do so.

We visited Mum on a regular basis and were able to monitor the care she received and the way in which she was treated. Sadly, other residents in care homes across the UK may not be lucky enough to have family close by and may have infrequent visitors, if any. These individuals are often not in a position to speak up for themselves and their families may be unaware of any issues surrounding their care and treatment. We have never been scared to challenge those we have trusted to care for our Mum and hope our experiences may encourage others to raise questions when the care system falls short of expectations or fails their loved ones. In our experience of adult social care in the UK, there are some excellent carers and care providers, but there are also some who do not meet the required standard.

Dos and Don'ts

Do:

- Be prepared to take matters further if Social Services and your local council are not willing or able to resolve matters. The next step, after approaching your local council, is to contact the Local Government and Social Care Ombudsman (see Useful Contacts at the end of this book).

Facts and Figures

- Research carried out by Dr Caroline Green and Professor Jill Manthorpe at King's College London, in May 2023, revealed that at least 5,871 care home residents in England were served with a 'notice to quit' between September 2021 and October 2022 (King's College London).

Chapter 14
Dad's Final Days

Our dad died in 2005, after a short illness. He became unwell with flu, just before Christmas 2004 and struggled to shake it off. He remained in bed and Mum looked after him, giving him the very best care. He had suffered all his life with bronchitis and this time it turned to pneumonia.

In the New Year, he was taken into our local hospital and expected to recover. He hadn't been there long when we visited to find him unable to speak properly. He was slurring his words and not making any sense. We asked a nurse why he couldn't talk, and the reply was, 'Oh, is that unusual then? We thought he always talked like that.' It transpired Dad had suffered a stroke, but no one at the hospital had realised.

The stroke damaged his oesophagus, so when Dad tried to eat, food would go down his windpipe, causing him to choke. The damage couldn't be repaired and, coupled with the pneumonia, he was very unwell. The situation escalated quickly and we were told there was little they could do for him. He was moved to a different ward, which we dubbed 'Death Row' as it seemed to be where patients with no hope were sent to die. It felt like a depressing way to end your life.

Dad was put on the controversial Liverpool Care Pathway (LCP) – a programme for delivering palliative care to people with a terminal illness, which basically deprives them of food and water. It seemed unnecessarily cruel to us. Mum was understandably very distressed but she came from a generation who didn't question the doctor's word, and didn't want to make a fuss. As there wasn't any hope of Dad recovering, we put our trust in the medical profession that this was the right thing to do. We have thought about it a great deal since. It really wasn't!

All the nursing team could do was to keep Dad comfortable and make sure he didn't suffer. Many of the nurses were fantastic, including one particular nurse who was very attentive and caring and always willing to chat and share a joke. Others less so. Dad's mouth was supposed to be swabbed regularly to avoid it becoming too dry, and he was allowed a little ice to suck on. However, staff often forgot to do this. When challenged, one nurse said she hadn't been told this during handover but we quickly pointed to Dad's notes where it was clearly written. Dad also had a catheter which sometimes became unattached and we would find him in a wet bed. He would press the buzzer for attention but the nurses were always busy and often slow to respond.

Between us we took turns at Dad's bedside, dividing day and evening visits to fit in with family life and work. As much as possible, one of us would try to be with Mum at Dad's bedside, at all times. Dad was remarkably upbeat and accepting. He knew he was dying and would never leave the hospital, although we tried to convince him otherwise. At times, he would say funny things and have strange visions, which we assumed was down to the medication he was taking, although his obsession with clocks and time seemed to suggest he was counting down to something only he knew about.

Having spent all those hours, days and weeks with him, he passed away when we weren't present. But that was just like Dad, not wanting a fuss. We had been told by the medical team that we had more time, and it was a shock when the call came in the night to say he was fading fast. Sadly, we arrived too late, but we had silently said goodbye many times while he was in hospital. It was better for him not to go on suffering.

We understand that, since 2014, the LCP is no longer routinely used - thank goodness - and patients are allowed a more dignified end to their lives. We didn't feel it was fully explained or that we were given any choice and have subsequently found out that many hospitals at that time were offered cash incentives to achieve targets for the number of patients on the LCP. How appalling and inhuman is that? We lost faith in the system and it taught us to always question decisions that were being made for a loved one. Both of us felt there was cause for complaint but Mum was too upset at the time to cope with pursuing it. As we mourned Dad, we vowed that, when the time came, we would make sure our Mum received better treatment. And we tried very hard to keep that promise.

Chapter 15
Pandemic

At the beginning of 2020, a new threat to Mum's well-being entered our lives, although as we celebrated the start of a new decade we remained happily ignorant about what was to come.

In December 2019, in Wuhan, the capital of Central China's Hubei province, the first cases of a new virus were beginning to emerge and, by the end of the month, Chinese health authorities were already dealing with substantial numbers of sick people. On the 11th of January, the first official death was reported, a sixty-one-year-old man. Throughout January more incidences were recorded in other countries, and on the 20th of January 2020, The World Health Organization (WHO) declared a global health emergency. Coronavirus had arrived. (COVID-19 is an acronym that stands for Coronavirus Disease 2019.)

By February the disease had emerged in Italy but it took a while for the seriousness of the situation to reach UK shores and even longer for our government to act. In late February, Kim celebrated her birthday and can remember being in London enjoying a pre-theatre lunch and washing her hands, over and over, in the washroom, while singing 'Happy Birthday to me'. In the early days, we were told good hand hygiene would be enough to keep the disease at bay and washing your hands for the length of time it took to sing the lyrics of 'Happy Birthday' twice through was advised. At that time, this seemed amusing. No one yet appreciated the seriousness of the situation.

Meanwhile, Sue and Brian were on holiday in Thailand. They had been monitoring the COVID-19 situation carefully before deciding that it would be safe to travel, based on government guidance at that time. While they were away the UK government added Thailand to the very small list of countries that required people returning from those destinations to isolate for two weeks on their return home. This meant that Sue was unable to visit Mum until late March, when Care Home 2 was already discontinuing visits. She was allowed just half an hour with Mum before the doors were closed to visitors. Having been so actively involved in Mum's life, it was a shock to suddenly find ourselves shut out.

Our family had been looking forward to a big celebration for Mark's 60th birthday, to take place over the Easter holidays in early April. Friends and family were due to travel from around the country to help Mark celebrate this landmark occasion. The venue had been booked, food and drink organised and Mark had been practising his DJ set for several months. Everything was prepared. There was no way this creeping threat could impact the party, or so we believed.

The situation escalated quickly. Throughout March the world watched in horror at the devastating effects of COVID-19 as it spread rapidly in Italy. In the worst affected areas the Italian health service struggled to cope as the casualties literally piled up. It was humbling and frightening. Travel bans, closures and lockdowns were announced around the globe as the world struggled to contain this new virus that was believed to have originated in a Chinese wet market thousands of miles away.

In the UK, the government was slow to respond to the coming crisis. It was obvious to us, and many people, that not acting quickly enough would prove disastrous and cost many lives. Shouting at the TV as politicians delayed and repeatedly failed to act became the norm.

The situation in Italy had, by this time, become extremely serious. Italy was a lot closer to home than China, and the virus was now spreading in near neighbours Spain and France. The elderly appeared to be particularly impacted by COVID-19 and we were beginning to feel an increasing uneasiness as reports of outbreaks among residents in UK care homes were reported.

As the month progressed, it became apparent the planned party could not go ahead, even if such an event was allowed. We had to do the responsible thing and postpone. At the start of March we had been fussing over such trivial priorities as party outfits and decorations but by the time of Mark's birthday we were preparing to stay at home and wait out a global pandemic.

One by one, our freedoms were withdrawn and our lives shrunk. On the 18th of March it was announced that UK schools were to close and Kim's son, Sam, reluctantly returned home from university. Hasty plans were made for everyone to work from home and bedrooms doubled up as offices. This was to be followed closely by the closure of pubs, restaurants, gyms and other venues.

On the 23rd of March, the then UK prime minister, Boris Johnson, addressed the nation, in the first of what were to become familiar bulletins by the government, and announced the first full national lockdown. UK citizens could only go outside to buy food and to exercise once a day, unless they couldn't work from home. The message was 'Stay Home, Protect the NHS, Save Lives'. The doors of Care Home 2 were already closed to visitors and now, along with care homes across the UK, they had a government mandate to remain shut for the foreseeable future.

Without doubt, the UK government was unprepared for a global pandemic. Care Home 2, like many others, had no suitable equipment when Covid-19 hit; nothing! There was a shortage of masks and they had no way of sourcing them, as their usual suppliers quickly ran out of stock due to increased demand. Then, when a shipment of masks did arrive, they were out of date and a danger to carers' health, this information being received too late to prevent them being used and putting carers at risk. In the early days, with no access to the recommended full Personal Protective Equipment (PPE) staff were forced to wear bin liners to afford some kind of protection.

The NHS was under extreme pressure from the number of people becoming sick with COVID-19 and requiring hospital care. This meant there was no guarantee if or when medical help would be available for care home residents – with or without COVID. If a resident had a fall or became ill for another reason, there were no assurances when they might be seen. And if they were taken into hospital, there was a risk of infection from COVID. An ITV movie, *Help* (2021), starring Jodie Comer and Stephen Graham, would later depict the desperate situation faced by many carers with staff often left to cope alone, dialling 999 and receiving little or no assistance. We have subsequently been told this was a fairly accurate account of how things were at the time.

Funerals took place without mourners, or with heavily restricted numbers. During lockdown, if a loved one died, due to COVID or another reason, family and friends were largely unable to attend their funeral. The deceased were buried or cremated without their loved ones and families could only grieve in private.

In Care Home 2, and other care settings, staff were working long hours, often doing six nights a week to cover staff shortages through sickness and resignations. Some staff would fail to show up for shifts as they were too afraid of catching the disease and passing it on, putting more pressure on those who remained. Carers were tired, fearful and drained. They felt forgotten and alone. Yet, still they continued to care for our loved ones.

From the outset, there was a lack of leadership, support and coherent policies from UK government. Promises were made and then retracted (and, apparently, this continues at the time of writing). Information should be passed to care homes through The Health Protection Team but during the pandemic care home managers were finding out the latest developments from the media, along with everyone else. They were not given time or resources to implement changes and advise residents and their families what was happening.

The manager and staff at Care Home 2 fought hard to protect their residents, often with carers putting themselves at risk to shop in supermarkets as their usual supply chains had dried up. At first, supermarkets did not prioritise care homes for delivery slots. Later, our local council arranged for a large supermarket chain to make half hour slots available, but these could only be accessed at midnight by staff who were already exhausted from working long shifts in a difficult and stressful situation.

In spite of these challenges, we were confident Mum was in safe hands at Care Home 2 and would be well-looked after for what would, surely, be a short period of time while this horrible disease was brought under control. Modern medicine can provide an answer for many health emergencies and we prayed science would find a way. We put our lives in the hands of health and key workers and clapped every Thursday to show our gratitude ('Clap for Carers' and later 'Clap for Heroes' was a united show of appreciation, whereby the UK population would go outside and applaud at 8.00 pm every Thursday, instigated by Annemarie Plas). We couldn't help thinking a pay rise and better working conditions would be more appropriate. In our opinion, NHS and care staff were, and remain, underpaid and undervalued.

At this point, Mum's health had been relatively stable for around a year, since her arrival and initial improvement at Care Home 2. However, the fact that she suffered from Alzheimer's disease made communication extremely difficult during lockdown. She could not hold a phone unaided or talk for long periods, if at all. Like many residents, she had no understanding whatsoever about the pandemic and why the familiar and reassuring faces of the care home staff had all disappeared behind face masks and visors.

While Mum's physical needs were being addressed and she was well-fed and comfortable, like thousands of others, the lockdown and subsequent COVID-19 restrictions were to have a devastating effect on her mental health. Already in the grip of dementia, lack of contact would exact a toll. Not only were regular visits from family members brought to an end but so too were those of the hairdresser, chiropodist and other visitors who would all engage with residents during the course of an average week.

The care home was busy and had several residents and their families to consider and calls were limited to once a day. Between us, we alternated in phoning the home and, at best, would manage a few precious minutes trying to talk to Mum. It was heart-breaking not to be able to see her, hug her, kiss her and talk to her in the way we were used to. On a good day, she might manage a feeble 'I love you', on a bad day she would be withdrawn or sleepy. If the latter occurred, it would be a worrying twenty-four hours before one of us could attempt to speak to her again. Sometimes, a few days would pass without any proper contact. We tried to remain optimistic. Mum was strong and the restrictions surely couldn't last beyond a few weeks!

Living in lockdown was a strange experience. The country was much quieter with less traffic on the roads and fewer trains running. Pubs, restaurants, clubs, cinemas and gyms were all closed and the usually busy seafront, close to our homes, was silent. There were temporary shortages of certain food items and some essentials, such as flour and toilet roll, and we wrote to Mum (the carers would read our letters to her) and told her that we were being given a small glimpse of some aspects of life in wartime such as rationing. Back then, in the Second World War, people put their lives in danger for their country, whereas we had simply been told to 'stay at home'. (Even this was too much for some people!) We tried to explain to her about the virus, likening it to a flu epidemic, but she had no idea what it was all about. The only thing that mattered to Mum was being deprived of her family. It must have felt like we had abandoned her.

Hugging, kissing and touching were understandably banned with people outside of your household. Yet, Mum had always responded to our touch. This is not the case for everyone who suffers from dementia (and Mum didn't like being handled in general or any change in routine). There were many days, pre-COVID, when we would sit with her and just hold her hand. Her eyes may have been closed and conversation was poor, but she would squeeze our fingers if we tried to pull our hands away. She always knew we were there and this obviously gave her comfort. On a better day, we would be able to hold or cuddle her and she seemed to enjoy this closeness. When even these simple acts were banned, Mum would gradually withdraw into herself.

Singing at public gatherings was also forbidden. And, as previously mentioned, Mum loved to sing. Before she went into care she would join in enthusiastically on trips to the theatre, including inappropriate moments such as in the cinema watching a musical. Whenever singing in public was required, we sisters would betray our maternal heritage (several of Mum's brothers and sisters had good singing voices, and one of our uncles was a member of the Harrogate Choral Society, along with his lovely wife, both now sadly deceased), and join in badly. The staff at Care Home 2 always made sure Mum was able to listen to her CDs. She enjoyed Katherine Jenkins, Alfie Boe, Frank Sinatra, Sarah Brightman and Andrea Bocelli, along with all the tunes from favourite musicals, past and present. As we said earlier, music can have a transformative effect on those suffering from dementia, particularly songs from the person's past, and Mum would always respond, tapping her hand or feet in time to the beat, even when her eyes were closed. Sadly, in just a short time, Mum's life would be reduced to four walls and a CD player.

Even Prime Minister Boris Johnson would succumb to COVID-19 and spend time in St Thomas' Hospital in intensive care. At the beginning of April 2020, global cases passed one million, and in the UK, for the first time, nearly 1,000 deaths were recorded from the disease in one day. COVID-19 testing, which had been rudimentary at the start, was ramped up and new phrases entered the public conscience such as 'social distancing', 'flattening the curve' and 'contact tracing' (an app that alerted individuals if they had been in contact with anyone who had COVID).

The 75th anniversary of VE Day fell on the 8th of May 2020. Many planned events across the UK had to be cancelled or scaled down due to lockdown. The Red Arrows soared above the English skies, reminding us of many happy times spent with Mum at the Southend-on-Sea Airshow in years gone by. In Care Home 2, the carers did their best to mark the occasion and residents' families were sent a video of their loved ones. We have a lovely picture of Mum from this time; sitting in her comfy chair, a Union Jack flag in one hand, a scone and jam in the other. She looked tired, but well and happy. Our hearts broke.

In mid-May, after nearly two months of lockdown, the government set out a plan to re-open society and the message changed to 'Stay Alert, Control the Virus, Save Lives' (whatever 'stay alert' meant - as if we could actually see the virus in the air or on people). We allowed ourselves to be hopeful. The worst was over. The 'curve' had been flattened. We looked forward to being able to visit our mum again. Sadly, this would not happen for some time to come.

Dos and Don'ts

Do:

- Contact your care provider, in the event of an emergency, about the best way to receive updates on what is happening in your care home, and how to communicate with your loved one.

Don't:

- Forget that, while social media might not be the best way to source reliable information in an emergency situation, it can be a good way to contact local support groups and find out about help available in your area.

Facts and Figures

- The COVID-19 outbreak was officially declared a pandemic by WHO in March 2020.
- As of August 2023, over six and a half million people worldwide have died from COVID-19 (WHO).

Chapter 16
A New Chapter

After Dad died, we rallied round to support Mum. Again, she surprised us with her strength of character and, having never lived on her own before, managed extremely well. Initially, the biggest problem was loneliness and we visited as often as we could. We would go over for lunch and Mum would always have a ham and tomato sandwich on brown bread, something she would ask for even when we took her out to eat at one of her favourite local restaurants or cafes. She never did like 'fancy' food and preferred straightforward home cooking.

Mum was a good cook, but not very adventurous, preferring a 'meat and two veg' dinner over curry (which she had cooked for Dad through the years, but never ate). When she first moved to the town, she would shop regularly at the local bakers, butchers and greengrocers, until the arrival of a large supermarket chain that saw many businesses closing in the name of progress. However, Mum always preferred to prepare a meal using fresh ingredients.

For many years, when Dad was alive, he grew his own vegetables. He had turned half of the garden into a vegetable plot and it was not uncommon in those days to leave the house with bags of tomatoes, radishes, beetroot or runner beans. He was fairly successful, probably because once he retired, he would be out there every day, tending to his plants. He produced vegetables from his small patch for many years until it became too much for him, and the garden was laid to lawn. When Dad passed, family members helped out with mowing and heavier jobs, but Mum would still maintain pots of colourful plants outside the kitchen window.

For years, Dad had also made his own wine and the kitchen would frequently be full of demijohns, syphons, bottles, corks and all manner of winemaking paraphernalia. It was fairly potent too, and again, he would be generous in pouring out a glass of his latest batch, or sending us home with a bottle or two of elderflower wine. This hobby ceased long before Mum was widowed but we found some of the equipment, years later, when we were preparing the house to rent. All these memories surrounded and sustained Mum as she faced life without Dad.

Away from home, we took Mum on days out, further afield. One of the most memorable trips was to Buckingham Palace. When Queen Elizabeth II opened up part of her house to visitors, Mum said that she would very much like to go. Undaunted by the many challenges this presented, we duly booked tickets.

Aside from the two of us and Mum, our small party included three of Mum's grandchildren; Emily, Chloe and Sam. We travelled by train to London, taking a wheelchair for Mum so that we could push her round the palace. This was back in the days before it became too uncomfortable for her. We organised a large, private taxi to meet us at the station and Mum really enjoyed looking out of the window at the London sights. Our journey took us alongside the River Thames, past the London Eye, which we had taken Mum on during a previous trip, and St Thomas's Hospital where Emily and Chloe had been born. Then it was across Westminster Bridge, past Big Ben and the Houses of Parliament and on to 'Buck House'.

On arrival at the visitors' entrance, to our surprise, we were told there was no wheelchair access (at least, at that time). However, the friendly staff advised us that someone would meet us and let us in at the front gates. So, we quickly wheeled Mum round to the front of Buckingham Palace where, sure enough, we were let in through one of the famous gates.

We were met by a lovely lady who treated Mum as if she was the Queen herself. We piled into a little buggy and were driven up to an entrance door. The area was packed with tourists who were surprised and intrigued to see the small group being escorted through the gates of Buckingham Palace and driven up to the door, and we had attracted quite a crowd. Our mum, bless her, being of similar age to Her Majesty and bearing more than a passing resemblance, began to give the royal wave. The cameras outside the gates began clicking... We still laugh at the thought of unknowing tourists proudly showing off their photos of 'Her Majesty The Queen' taken on that day.

As we have said before, Mum loved to sing and enjoyed dancing and music so, over the years, we took her to see many concerts and plays. We are lucky enough to live close to two excellent local theatres and have been able to see some amazing West End productions on tour, as well as pantomimes and local productions.

One of the last shows we took Mum to see was particularly memorable; *Fiddler on the Roof* starring Paul Michael Glaser of seventies' hit TV series *Starsky and Hutch,* who played Perchik. We had allowed plenty of time and arranged a wheelchair taxi to take Mum in comfort to the theatre. However, as was often the case when a wheelchair was involved, the taxi was extremely late. So late, in fact, we risked missing the start of the performance. We contacted the theatre and explained to the staff who assured us we would be allowed in. Luckily, the performance was delayed for a few minutes. We raced into the auditorium with red faces, pushing Mum, just as the curtain was about to rise. It was an excellent performance and we are so glad we didn't miss any of it.

On another trip to London, we went to a carol concert at the Royal Albert Hall, enjoying a wonderful evening. Earlier in the day, we visited Harrods department store in Knightsbridge where we bought souvenirs and spent a long time in the magnificent food halls, sampling caviar and Champagne (well, we girls did). Being Christmas time, the famous store was beautifully decorated and had all kinds of festive treats. Mum was particularly proud of her new Harrods shopping bag.

Mum was partial to tea and cake (who isn't?) and loved it when we took her to The Ritz Hotel in Mayfair to indulge in a fancy afternoon tea. The 'tea' comprised of a selection of finger sandwiches; scones, jam and cream; and a choice of different teas or coffee. Everything was served on elegant bone china in luxurious surroundings and it was a pleasant way to while away an afternoon. Later, when it became too difficult for Mum to travel to London, we arranged similar teas closer to home and some of them were very good, but nothing quite compared to the opulence of The Ritz.

Chapter 17
Locked Out

Towards the end of May 2020, the WHO warned that the pandemic was far from over, despite many countries easing lockdowns and restrictions. In England, society continued to open up with groups of up to six people allowed to meet outside from the 1st of June, while maintaining social distancing (2 metres apart); warmer days were here and everyone felt more optimistic.

By this time, there had been many outbreaks of COVID-19 in care homes and numerous deaths. At the beginning of the pandemic, elderly residents were often discharged from hospital into care homes without being tested for COVID-19, something the manager at Care Home 2 would not do, refusing to take in new residents without a negative COVID test, protecting the vulnerable adults already in her care. We were grateful to her and the staff for keeping our mother safe. We knew Mum was in good hands at Care Home 2, where staff affectionately called her 'Nanny Jean', but it did not reduce the gnawing ache of effectively being excluded from her life.

The disease was much more dangerous to the elderly and vulnerable and it was right to protect them, but as time rolled on, we began to question this decision. We were not alone. Families across the UK were asking the same thing. When will we be allowed to see our loved ones? Again, government guidelines were often contradictory and confusing and care homes appeared to be low down on their list of priorities.

Early summer brought more fine weather and people were relieved to be allowed to visit parks and tourist spots. Crowds of people rushed to popular locations and the local beaches were packed. We kept well away, mindful of the need to protect ourselves and Mum, in particular, for when we were allowed in. We followed the rules and guidance and waited in frustration for care homes to open up to visitors.

Lockdown restrictions continued to ease in the UK, but not in care homes. It was decided that visits to care homes could only safely take place outside and was limited to two regular family members. Work began at Care Home 2 to construct a visiting pod in their large garden. In the meantime, visits were facilitated under a gazebo on the patio, with the resident one side of the table and up to two visitors on the other. The carers had been wearing full PPE from the outset but that summer, wearing masks in shops and enclosed places became mandatory for all. Even though our visits were outside, we were expected to wear a mask.

In late June, we set off together to see Mum for the first time in months. It was a sunny day and, although very frail, for once Mum didn't seem to be too uncomfortable sitting in a wheelchair. It had become more and more difficult to take her out, prior to the pandemic. Severe arthritis in her shoulders made it painful for her to sit in the confined space and she was finding it increasingly difficult to lift her head. Her comfy, electric recliner armchair was cumbersome to move around or take outside, hence necessitating a wheelchair on this occasion. Mum was in good spirits and very happy to see us. It was lovely to sit outside with her and chat, although frustrating not to be able to hold her hand or give her a hug. She also couldn't understand why we had to wear a mask and thought we were just being difficult by refusing to take them off (resulting in a proper telling off!). We were allowed to stay for just under an hour but felt a bit more positive about visits in future.

However, the two subsequent garden visits didn't go at all well. Mum was obviously uncomfortable, fidgety and in pain, and quickly asked to go back inside. We tried hard to distract her and persuade her to stay outside for a short while to talk to us, but it was obviously not going to work. A carer came and wheeled her back inside, but Mum expected us to be able to follow. It was distressing, as we were leaving, to hear her calling for us. We left with heavy hearts and tears in our eyes.

It was around this time we received the final, much delayed, decision from the LGO. The Final Judgement found in our favour in almost all points. We had won our case. We were elated that someone had finally acknowledged the wrongs that had been done to Mum and our family. Care Home 1 and the local council were instructed to improve their practices. We hoped this might help someone else's family in the future and prevent them from suffering the same treatment and injustice. We vowed to celebrate with Mum at the first opportunity. (Mum was unaware of the case with the LGO, as by now she lacked the necessary cognitive skills, but we hoped to share our success, on her behalf, with her in some way. Sadly, this would never happen.)

In August, the UK government launched their 'Eat Out to Help Out' offering a 50% discount on meals up to £10 a person. The scheme was intended to encourage people back to restaurants and cafes, although only in small groups with social distancing. We sisters were able to meet at a local café and enjoy lunch outside for the first time in many months. Naturally, our thoughts were with Mum and how much she used to like going out to lunch.

Meanwhile, the situation in care homes seemed to be moving backwards. Window visits replaced garden visits. Initially we were able to visit together, once a week, but later we had to alternate as one visitor only was allowed at a time. The constantly changing guidelines were difficult for us to keep up with, so we can only imagine how hard it must have been for care home staff.

We were fortunate that Mum was now in a downstairs room with a window that looked out onto the side alley of the care home. (When she first arrived, her room was at the back of the building up two flights of stairs.) We were hopeful this might work. Sadly, this was to prove not to be the case. We were still expected to wear masks, even though we were outside, and Mum couldn't hear what we were saying very well. For safety reasons, the window would only open a fraction which didn't help. As previously mentioned, Mum was unable to lift her head very far and we couldn't make eye contact with her. As she was in, or on, her bed, it was not uncommon for her to sleep through the entire visit. These occasions were frustrating and extremely sad. We struggled on as warm sunny days were replaced with cooler autumnal ones. The whole summer with Mum had been lost to us.

In mid-October, a new three-tier system of COVID-19 restrictions was introduced in England. We were placed in a tier with fewer restrictions and, on the 12th of the month, when Kim arrived for her usual window visit, to her delight and surprise, she was allowed to go inside the care home to visit Mum in her bedroom. It meant wearing full PPE including an apron, mask, visor and gloves but she could hold Mum's hand and have a cup of tea with her.

Unfortunately, around this time, one of Sue's sons contracted COVID and, although he didn't live with her, she had to stay away from the care home for two weeks to be on the safe side. Kim, therefore, managed a second visit with Mum, although this time it felt different. The staff appeared to be more nervous and uneasy, and the visit was for a shorter time. The warm summer months had provided a hiatus but cases of COVID-19 were on the rise in the UK once more. Sue would manage just one more inside visit before the doors to care homes were, once again, closed to visitors.

Up close, the deterioration in Mum was more obvious. She was sleepy and much more withdrawn. This was partly due to the advancement of Alzheimer's disease but we believe it was also due to the lack of stimulation and contact with loved ones. We knew that the carers talked to Mum, but she missed her family. And we missed her. By this point, Mum had not seen her grandchildren and great-grandchildren since the early part of the year.

Around this time, she also began to spend much more time in her room, partly because she was undoubtedly more comfortable but also so the care home could protect those, like Mum, who were particularly vulnerable. We were glad that she was being well cared for but desperately sad that she now spent so many hours in bed.

The year had brought about a decline in Mum and all we could do was watch through a window and hope that restrictions would lift so that we could spend more time with her – before time ran out.

Facts and Figures

- In 2020/21 the Ombudsman received 11,830 complaints and enquiries from members of the public in spite of being closed to new complaints during the first COVID-19 lockdown. During that same period, the Ombudsman upheld 67% of investigations, a greater proportion than ever before (Local Government and Social Care annual review 2020/21).
- During 2020/21, the Ombudsman issued 1,488 recommendations for councils to improve their services for others, such as revising procedures and training staff. These findings suggest systemic problems with local government services, as opposed to one-off mistakes. (Source as above.)

Chapter 18
A Good Sport

Mum always enjoyed sport. Her particular favourite was tennis, which she had played in her younger years, and athletics, although she would watch any competitive match or game, more often than not cheering on the supposed underdog. She was enthusiastic about the London Marathon, the Great North Run and the annual Oxford/Cambridge boat race, among other sporting fixtures. She would even watch snooker – one of the sports enjoyed by Dad. Two occasions we remember well are the 2006 World Cup and the 2013 Wimbledon Men's Singles Final when Andy Murray took the title.

June 2006 saw the start of World Cup fever. On the 10th of June 2006 England played Paraguay. The match fell a few days after Brian's sixtieth birthday, so a family party was arranged in honour of the occasion. England flags flew and banners saying 'Come on England' were hung up. Invites were sent out requesting all guests wear the obligatory red and white of the England football team. It made Mum happy to see all the family there, dressed in hats, wigs, football shirts and tops. Mum got into the spirit of things, as usual, dressing up and wearing a rather striking red and white wig.

Everyone piled into the lounge, jostling for position in front of the TV. Drinks were served pre-match as nerves kicked in. Then they were off. There was lots of shouting, whoops and cries of 'oh no'. When the final whistle went, England had won 1-0. It didn't seem to matter that it was due to an own goal by Paraguay. We had won and were through to the next round. As far as everyone was concerned there was a lot to celebrate; a sixtieth birthday and a World Cup match win. There was a lot of dancing and Mum enjoyed every moment with her family and close friends. (England subsequently lost to Portugal in the quarter finals, after the match went to penalties [3-1 to Portugal]. Italy went on to lift the coveted FIFA World Cup trophy that year.)

Each year, for as far back as we can remember, we would watch as many of the big tennis matches as possible with Mum including, of course, Wimbledon. In the year a British player took the title for the first time since Fred Perry lifted the famous trophy, seventy-seven years previously, we naturally helped Mum to cheer him on. We made our own cream tea with scones, jam and strawberries and refilled the kettle several times during the tense, three set match, when Murray beat Novak Djokovic in straight sets (6–4, 7–5, 6–4). Mum loved every moment and it was so good to celebrate a British victory, something we had failed to manage in football for many years. At least Mum and Dad got to see the famous (and, to date, only) England World Cup win, back in 1966! How she would have loved watching the Lionesses bring home the Women's Euro 2022 trophy.

Closer to home, Mum was always very proud of all her grandchildren's sporting achievements from a win in the sack race on school sports day to their various successes in football, running, dancing, swimming and horse riding.

One year on holiday on the south coast at a well-known holiday camp, Mum achieved her own small sporting victory. A good sport, as always, she joined in the grandmothers' egg and spoon race. We all cheered as Mum ran to an easy win, but she was nearly disqualified because they said she looked too young and glamorous to be a grandma (she was, by then, nan to Nick and Gareth). She quickly put them straight (Mum could be very forthright and straight talking) and won a small prize but was secretly much more chuffed about the compliment.

That same holiday, Dad accompanied Kim on a hack organised by the camp. The leader asked if anyone had ridden before and, naturally, Dad said yes, saying he was a good rider, having learnt to ride horses at the barracks as a child. A skill you never forget, apparently! They then led out this magnificent black stallion that, from the look in his eyes, would much rather have remained in his nice warm stable, eating hay, and handed the reins to Dad. We mounted our steeds and followed the leader out of the paddock, single file. It was a gentle hack, until we reached the open fields and the lead horse began to trot. Our well-trained mounts obediently followed. All except for the black stallion who shot past at a gallop with Dad grimly holding on. Dad eventually managed to bring the horse under control and trotted back to the stunned, now stationary, group. 'I told you I could ride,' he said, but we had a good chuckle and never let him forget the incident.

Although she loved to watch sport, Mum didn't participate in later life, and kept fit mainly through walking. Not being able to drive, she would walk everywhere. Long before it was fashionable and the fitness industry persuaded us to purchase expensive trainers and fancy leggings, Mum would put on a pair of sensible shoes and her regular clothes and head outdoors. And she walked fast; it was hard to keep up, even for the younger ones. She must have covered many thousands of miles in her lifetime and always at a pace. Maybe that was one of the reasons her heart remained healthy and strong, allowing her to live to such a good age, long after her mind had begun to play tricks on her.

Chapter 19
Hope and Despair

Throughout late autumn 2020, the Scientific Advisory Group for Emergencies (SAGE) debated with the UK government over whether the substantial rise in cases warranted imposing another lockdown. SAGE provides independent scientific advice to the government during a time of national emergency with members being drawn from a number of scientific disciplines headed by the Chief Medical Officer and the Government Chief Scientific Adviser. (At the time these positions were held by Professor Sir Chris Whitty and Sir Patrick Vallance respectively. Both were appointed Knight Commander of the Order of the Bath [KCB] in the 2022 New Year Honours List for their services during the pandemic.)

SAGE was concerned about the first of a succession of new variants of COVID-19, originating in South East England, the Kent variant (which later became known as the Alpha variant), as it spread more easily. Therefore, on the 5th of November, a second (one month) lockdown began in England to curb the numbers of those infected in the run up to Christmas, and reduce pressure on a struggling NHS. During this period we had little contact with Mum.

The staff at Care Home 2 did their best to help maintain relationships between the residents and their families. Around this time, we received a letter from Mum that the carers had helped her to compose (with them doing the writing). Although obviously dictated, we could hear Mum's voice in the words. The letter said how proud Mum was of us both and how much she looked forward to being able to see us again. It was painful for us to read, knowing we were still unable to visit.

When restrictions were eased at the beginning of December, and the tier system reintroduced, care homes largely remained closed to visitors. By this time families were anxious and angry, having not been able to see their loved ones for the best part of a year. National campaigns, such as Rights for Residents, were set up to pressurise the government into allowing named visitors into care homes to visit their relatives and friends. We signed petitions and joined in the debate on social media. A growing sense of urgency and collective unease was felt by anyone with a relative in a care home. It was as though our loved ones had been locked away and forgotten. For many, it was already too late with mums, dads and grandparents dying alone, from COVID-19 and other causes, without the comfort of family around them. Many people were denied the chance to say goodbye. We had already travelled a long journey with Mum; surely it couldn't end this way without us having an opportunity to see her?

Then Prime Minister Boris Johnson announced that up to three households would be able to meet during a five-day Christmas period (23rd to the 27th of December), depending on which tier you were in. We were in Tier 2 at that time, and therefore allowed to form a 'bubble' with three other households. Even so, it was doubtful that we would be able to see Mum, but remained hopeful, limiting our contact with everyone, even close family, so that we would be safe to visit if the opportunity arose.

Throughout the pandemic, scientists across the globe had been working to develop a vaccine. There was a race to be the first and, in late 2020, several companies had reached the testing phase. At the beginning of December, the first COVID-19 vaccine, developed by pharmaceutical giant Pfizer, was approved for use in the UK giving hope for life beyond the virus. The UK government set out the order of precedence for vaccination with Mum falling into a high priority category. We held our breath and dared to hope we might be able to see her soon.

Mum's birthday came round again and we hoped, against the odds, that we might be allowed in to the care home to see her. This did not happen and it was the first year as far back as we could remember that we had not celebrated with her. Falling a week before Christmas, her birthday had always marked the start of our festive celebrations. But not this year, on what was to be her last birthday.

Birthday presents had to be handed to the care

home well in advance so that they could be sanitised to ensure that they were disease-free. It was frustrating and sad, standing on the doorstep with a parcel, knowing Mum was inside, and not being allowed to cross the threshold. Mum loved fresh flowers, particularly brightly-coloured chrysanthemums, irises and carnations, and we had always taken flowers when we visited, both at her home and in care homes. But flowers of any kind were now not allowed (the symptoms of hay fever brought on by the pollen in flowers could be mistaken for COVID-19). She also loved homemade cake. However, we could only send in shop-bought cake, instead of our usual homemade jam sponge, again to ensure the safety of residents. It felt as if everything, however small, that would bring her joy was gradually being denied.

Along with many others, we tried to remain optimistic about Christmas. Boris Johnson was determined to deliver his promise of a family Christmas for all. But COVID-19 didn't respect religious celebrations of any denomination and cases of the Kent (Alpha) variant continued to rise. The heavy death count increased and the misery continued. Our contact with Mum reverted to weekly FaceTime or solo window visits, neither of which was satisfactory.

Our area was recording high numbers of COVID-19 and it was obvious that Christmas get-togethers were likely to be cancelled. Yet again, the government stalled in making a decision. We waited and hoped, but it was not good news for us. On the 21st of December, London and the South East of England was placed in Tier 4, meaning we wouldn't get to spend any time with Mum over the entire Christmas period; her last (although we did not know that then). It also meant we couldn't spend time together as sisters and with extended family, and it was a quiet and subdued festive period. Having any kind of meaningful communication with Mum was now almost impossible.

As it happened, Christmas 2020 was cancelled for everyone with the government backtracking on promised freedoms over the festive period. This meant people across the UK had to cancel their plans at the last moment, and many people spent Christmas on their own or in very small family groups. Everyone felt the tightening grip of the pandemic. It was a Christmas few will forget.

In late December, it was announced that lateral-flow rapid testing would become available in care homes, so that carers and residents could be tested for COVID-19 twice weekly. This was in addition to the more accurate, weekly PCR test they were already receiving. This was good news and we hoped it would eventually translate into visitor testing to allow us in to see Mum.

In early January, a second vaccine, developed by Oxford/AstraZeneca, was approved for use in the UK and the vaccination rollout ramped up. On the 9th of January, Mum received her first dose of the two-dose

AstraZeneca vaccine. With this protection in place, and the availability of improved, regular testing, it surely wouldn't be long before we would be able to see her.

Health workers and carers were also among the first to be vaccinated. This was good news because it meant additional protection for those looking after residents and their families. However, there appeared to be some reluctance on the part of some carers. We had been prevented from seeing our loved ones for so long by this point, it seemed crazy to think Mum might now be more at risk from those caring for her than her family who were still excluded from her life.

Then, on the 6th of January, 2021, England went into another full lockdown. In truth, this made little difference to us as we were already living under the highest restrictions in an effort to stem the spread of yet another variant, Delta, first identified in India. However, this lockdown looked like it would be for much longer and despite the vaccination rollout and the availability of rapid testing, we were still locked out of Mum's life.

Around this time we began to consider our options. We even discussed the unthinkable; another move. But not to another care home as we had no concerns over the care Mum received at Care Home 2. We talked about the possibility of looking after Mum at home, so that we could be a part of her daily life. Neither of our houses were geared up to care for someone with Mum's needs, nor did either of us have the space. We didn't have the right equipment, wet rooms or downstairs bedrooms. At this point in the pandemic, grown-up children had also come back to live at home. Still, we thought about it. We had to weigh up the potential impact of a move, against how much longer restrictions might last. We knew it would be traumatic for Mum, but at least she would be able to spend her last weeks and months with those who love her. Had we known just how little time she had left, we wouldn't have hesitated.

Shortly afterwards, we began to make a special case for Mum under the 'end of life pathway'. By now, Mum was practically bedbound. She slept most of the time and was much more withdrawn. It seemed obvious to us that she was beginning to fade. As we understood it, the end of life pathway would have allowed both of us to visit Mum in, what we felt sure were, the last weeks of her life, regardless of current restrictions. We had read that this access could be allowed for up to one year as a person neared the end. Sadly, at that time, our request was denied.

We continued to phone the home on a daily basis, although we rarely got to talk to Mum. She was either asleep or the overstretched carers were too busy. This situation was frustrating and distressing. All we could do was ask after her health and trust the carers to tell her that we had called when she was awake and give her our love.

Then, to make matters worse, we were told that calls would be limited to FaceTime once per week for each of us, due to the number of family members trying to contact residents. This was a real blow. A carer had to remain present with Mum to operate and hold the phone. They were always time-pressured and Mum was often asleep or, more worryingly, didn't want to talk to us at all. At best, this meant we had less than five minutes trying to communicate with Mum on a tiny screen once a week.

We were not alone. This situation was being played out in care homes across the country. It was never certain exactly who was responsible; the government, local councils or those in charge of the care homes. In truth, it seemed care home managers had to try and make sense of a great deal of ever-changing, confusing and contradictory advice. The authorities were all so terrified of COVID outbreaks, they seemed to lose sight of the bigger picture and the terrible toll being locked away from their families was having on residents.

It is obviously right to protect the most vulnerable in society, but we felt it shouldn't be at the expense of the comfort gained from seeing their loves ones in their final weeks and months. This amounts to cruelty of the worst kind. Many families lost elderly relatives during this time, unable to be with them at their passing. Elderly men and women passed away alone, confused and frightened, and not just those who sadly died from COVID-19. It was a horrible situation to find ourselves in, once again, caught in the middle, fighting for Mum's human rights.

Kim's birthday this year was a much more subdued

affair and, by this time, everyone was fed up with being locked down. The (rather grand) visiting pod at Care Home 2 was finally finished but proved to be little help to us, even when lockdown began to ease at the beginning of March, as Mum could not sit comfortably in a wheelchair and there was no other way of getting her out to the pod. Throughout February, we had virtually no contact with Mum.

Then regulations changed to allow one named visitor into care homes from the 8th of March. But only one! This meant families were forced to choose between them who should visit. For a number of reasons, we decided that Sue should be our named visitor. She had received her first COVID-19 vaccine some weeks before and had less contact with the outside world. She had also only been able to visit Mum once the previous autumn. It made sense for it to be her, still it was horrible having to make that decision as, throughout, we had been on this journey together.

Sue resumed inside visits and was allowed into Mum's bedroom to sit with her. She was required to have a rapid test for COVID-19 on the premises (in the aforementioned pod), and wear full PPE. Even then, visits were restricted to an hour at most, once a week. It was too little too late, and the deterioration in Mum was obvious. Once again, we appealed under the 'end of life pathway' and, this time, Kim was also able to visit, but again only weekly, for an hour at best.

Mother's Day fell on the 14th of March and no visitors were allowed into the majority of care homes.

This felt unkind and unnecessarily cruel. The situation in care homes, by now, was nothing short of a national tragedy. We were united with people across the country in the fight against what seemed to be a breach of human rights. We just wanted to spend time with our loved ones.

On Mother's Day, we received photos from staff at Care Home 2 of Mum being helped to open her presents; CDs, pyjamas, chocolates and a fake orchid (to get round the fresh flowers policy). Mum looked tired, not just in the physical sense but of life itself. For the first time, we felt she was giving up and it was more imperative than ever that we be allowed in to spend precious time with her.

We could see no justifiable reason why, with a negative test for COVID-19 and full PPE, we could not visit Mum more often. We were aware this would mean additional work for carers, who were already overworked and stressed, however, visitation should have been a government priority. Unfortunately, this never seemed to be the case. With Easter fast approaching, we once again asked about increasing visits, but to no avail.

On the 25th of March 2021, Sue visited Mum and was frustrated when her visit was curtailed by the arrival of a visitor to see another resident. Time was rationed and the unworkable guidelines were making it difficult for everyone. However, we could see that the light was fading in those familiar eyes and felt that time was fast running out for Mum.

Dos and Don'ts

Do:

- In the event of an emergency situation and you can't visit your loved one, try to keep the lines of communication open, no matter how difficult this might seem.

Don't:

- Give up, and if you find yourself blocked by the care provider, seek outside help and advice, such as Rights for Residents (see below).

Facts and Figures

- Rights For Residents was set up in September 2020 'in response to the cruel and inhumane visiting policies placed on care home residents'. The campaign quickly gathered momentum and has subsequently grown into a huge movement that continues to fight for the rights of people living in care and their families (Rights for Residents, 2023).

Chapter 20
Songs of Praise

Mum was brought up as a Methodist and was a regular churchgoer in her younger days. It tested Mum's faith greatly when she lost her longed-for babies, but it provided some comfort, too. Our dad was not at all religious, and she gradually moved away from the church, although she made sure both of her daughters attended Sunday School. Her faith must have had a big impact on her because often, when she was lost in the wilderness that is dementia, Mum would think she was in church. Maybe it provided an anchor, somewhere safe and familiar, or gave her comfort at some deep, subconscious level. We will never know for sure but the church was certainly a recurring theme while she was living in a care home.

Mum could always be relied on to sing enthusiastically to hymns at weddings, christenings and funerals and was often appalled that the younger generations could not be trusted to know the words without a hymn sheet. Our Sunday School upbringing ensured we could join in without visual prompts, albeit not tunefully. As mentioned before, Mum's family enjoyed singing and this was always a source of joy even at sad occasions like funerals. Regrettably, there have been many of those in recent years. It was bitter-sweet that Mum was the last of her siblings to depart this life and, when she died, the Morgan legacy passed to us and our cousins. Although living in different areas of the country, we have vowed to keep their memories alive and it was a great source of celebration when some of us were able to get together to celebrate one of our cousin's sixtieth birthday. It was a fabulous occasion with a marquee and a swing band. We're sure our parents would have loved it and were dancing with us on that day.

Mum always enjoyed *Songs of Praise,* which was broadcast on TV every Sunday evening. Mum would sing along while preparing tea, usually tinned salmon sandwiches (a favourite treat that she enjoyed well into her old age, while living at home). There was always a roast dinner at lunchtime on a Sunday, with two homemade desserts (apple crumble, egg custard, spotted Dick – though Mum refused to call it that on account that it sounded too rude!). There was often a conflict of interests on Sunday evenings as it aired the same night as *The Chart Show* was on the radio, a must for young teenagers.

After Dad died, Mum joined a Women's Group at the local Methodist church. She looked forward to the weekly meetings and would tell us about her friends there and the interesting speakers. Typical of Mum, she would frequently be found in the kitchen making tea for the group members or washing up. She would insist on walking the short distance there and back and it seemed to give her a real sense of achievement and purpose. Many of the ladies became close friends and it was a great loss when Mum moved into care and could no longer attend.

Naturally, we volunteered to drive her there but it was becoming much too difficult. She couldn't sit comfortably in the car like she used to (one of her favourite things was to be driven along the seafront and local area). She was also starting to find everything too confusing and it just wasn't safe to leave her unsupervised. However, in her mind, Mum would often return to the church setting and, as told in Chapter 11, she would even enjoy a sleepover there with her friends. What a lovely thought.

Chapter 21
Final Hours

The weekend following Sue's visit, Mum's health deteriorated very rapidly. She refused food and was reluctant even to take fluids. On Monday, the doctor was called in. Zara phoned us early in the morning to say Mum wasn't well and not responding to carers, and that we should both go in. We knew this was not good news. We rushed to the home to perform the necessary routine of COVID testing and putting on PPE, the first time we had been able to visit together since the previous summer under the gazebo.

We didn't move from Mum's bedside for the entire day, taking it in turns to sit beside her and hold her hand. She was largely unresponsive, but we talked to her constantly in the hope that she could hear us and know we were both there. She looked pale and frail and her breathing was irregular, sometimes rapid. Although she had been unwell before and rallied round many times, we knew this time was different. The doctor confirmed our fears and withdrew all medication. It was just a matter of time.

Mum looked comfortable and we were grateful that she was able to spend her final days and hours in a clean, comfy bed. She was surrounded by photos of her family; daughters, sons-in-law, grandchildren, great-grandchildren and newest arrival, her great-great-grandson, Alfie, who she would now sadly never meet (although we had forwarded photos and video clips – Mum never lost the sense of joy at the arrival of a new baby). There was so much love surrounding her in that room. Around that time, we read a quote somewhere that resonated with us as it was so true: 'If love could have saved her, she would have lived forever'.

We returned home briefly to our families for a rushed dinner, and went back to sit with Mum around 8.00 pm, staying until late as the nightshift staff worked silently around us. We debated whether or not to remain at her bedside through the night, but as there was no change and she looked peaceful, we were persuaded to go home for a few hours rest and return early the next morning.

After an anxious night, during which neither of us slept much, we rang Care Home 2 before 8.00 am and spoke to Zara. There was no change. So, we prepared ourselves for another precious day with Mum. However, sadly, this was not to be. Like our dad before her, the end was swift, and she died before we arrived. She went to sleep peacefully before we got there.

After a year of being locked out of Mum's life we had had just one last day with her. In some ways we considered ourselves to be lucky as many others had not even been granted this. But all those missed days, weeks and months of the past year took on huge significance. It is often said that loved ones wait for an opportunity to say goodbye, and maybe this was the case with Mum; she sat out those long, lonely months of lockdown and restrictions until we were able to be with her one last time. It still felt like a cruel blow.

Mum's extended family, grandchildren and great-grandchildren were devastated, having not been able to see her for over a year. Many tears were shed. But we took comfort from the fact this wonderful woman had been a part of our lives for so long and, even when we were locked out of her life, we were sure she knew how much she was loved. During the weeks between Mum's passing and the funeral, one month later, we were overwhelmed by the outpouring of love for her.

As restrictions were still in place, the funeral had to be limited to thirty people. Again, we felt fortunate as a few weeks earlier, numbers had been as low as six. Mum's funeral took place on the 29th of April, but just days before, on the 17th of April, 2021, The Queen (Elizabeth II) had made a sad and solitary figure, sitting alone in St George's Chapel, Windsor Castle, at the service for her beloved husband, Prince Philip (who died on the 9th April).

Given the situation in the UK, we didn't expect anyone to travel and it meant a great deal to us that some of our cousins were able to be with us on the day. We were, however, saddened that no one from Care Home 2 was able to attend due to continued caution over COVID, and it was a great shame that those who looked after Mum during the final year of her life were absent.

The coffin was covered in brightly-coloured flowers; that which Mum had been denied in life, we provided in abundance to mark her passing. Family and friends from Mum's long life were represented and it was a small intimate service in which everyone played a part. Her sons-in-law and some of her grandchildren were pallbearers and there were favourite hymns, poems and readings. Although we were limited by time, as well as numbers, we still considered ourselves fortunate to have been able to celebrate Mum's life with family and friends.

For the wake, we were allowed only fifteen, so had to limit numbers to close family. However, we were lucky enough to be able to make use of a marquee in the garden of a local pub where we enjoyed a late lunch. Just a short time before even limited gatherings like this had been banned.

The following day, the two of us took time to reflect as we distributed the many wreaths and bouquets to family graves and plots, including those of our dad and paternal grandparents. It was a poignant time, thinking about all those who have passed. We hope they have been reunited, that Mum is with family on both sides and is, once again, sharing a joke with our dad and her siblings.

Dos and Don'ts

Do:

- Find out if your loved one has any preferences in respect of their funeral and burial arrangements. They might wish to be buried close to family, be cremated or have a particular type of coffin. There may be favourite songs or hymns they would like to be played. When the time comes, it can be a comfort to know you are acting on your loved ones wishes.

Facts and Figures

- Nearly ten million people were unable to attend the funeral of someone they knew during lockdown. This figure is based on an estimate that 243,000 funerals went ahead in the UK during lockdown with an average of ten attendees due to COVID-19 rules, compared with fifty in normal times (Co-op Funeralcare study 2020).

Chapter 22
Dancing Still

Mum liked to be busy and took up different hobbies throughout her life. As mentioned before, she enjoyed knitting and would click away on her needles for hours on end, transforming colourful balls of wool into warm jumpers, scarves and, when the need arose, baby garments (another skill of Mum's we girls have not inherited!). In her younger days, she attended evening classes in sewing and ballroom dancing. Kim grew up wearing dresses and skirts made by Mum and was not always as appreciative as she might have been.

Although not exactly a hobby, Mum also liked to play card games, something she would happily join in with throughout her life. Christmas get-togethers and social occasions over the years would often end in a round of cards or other games. She was a demon at 'Pick-up Pairs', something to which all of her grandchildren will attest, so obviously had a sharp mind until Alzheimer's disease began to rob her of her memory. In later life, we encouraged her to play as a way of keeping her mind active but she would become frustrated when she couldn't remember like she used to.

Mum loved to dance. Unfortunately, our dad did

not share her passion and could rarely be persuaded onto the dancefloor, so Mum went to ballroom dancing lessons with a girl friend of hers, but it sounded like they always had a great time. This lady became a dear friend and Mum was sad when she moved away to be nearer to family. Now in her nineties, she still lives independently in the West Country. When Mum passed, we contacted her and had a lovely chat on the phone reminiscing about some of the stories from their dancing days.

Mum loved the TV show *Strictly Come Dancing*. Needless to say, we took her to see some of the dancers when they were performing at our local theatre. Another time, we attended a performance of Michael Flatley's *Riverdance* and Mum adored the Irish music and fancy footwork. Wherever she is now, we hope our lovely mum is still dancing.

Chapter 23
The Cost of it All

There was a huge price to pay for our experience of the adult social care system in the UK, both financial and emotional.

The financial costs of care are staggering and we found this side of things confusing at times and didn't feel our options were always properly explained to us by the local council. When Mum went into Care Home 1, the council carried out a financial assessment (means-test). In general the council will help to pay the cost of care if your savings fall below a certain amount (this amount being subject to change). As Mum owned her house, paid for by our grandparents and father through years of hard work, it was considered she should meet the full cost of her care. In Mum's case, the total amount to be paid by her was capped at a staggering £125,000 (the UK government has subsequently promised to reduce this).

As mentioned earlier, we rented out Mum's house and all of the income, plus her state and private pensions went towards the cost of her care. Even then, this didn't cover all the costs. We, therefore, arranged a deferred payment plan with the local council, against the property. This meant the remaining balance of the cost of care was deferred until such time as the house was sold. The numbers stacked up at an alarming rate.

When Mum was forced to leave Care Home 1, the costs increased as Care Home 2 was more expensive, even though Mum would be sharing a room. In truth, we were so relieved to have found somewhere safe for her to move to, where she would be properly looked after, we never paused to fully consider the financial aspect.

We were liable to cover the remainder of the costs as a 'third party top up'. We would gladly have done so, even though there was a worrying period of time while we looked at household budgets and considered how we might be able to meet the significant additional cost. The remortgaging of our homes was even discussed at one point, so daunting was the potential financial burden.

However, we then found out that this could be added to the deferred payment plan, although the council never told us this at the time and we had to find out for ourselves via Citizens Advice. The numbers continued to increase rapidly and, to be honest, the statements rarely made sense to us, designed, we suspected, to be confusing. At that time, we were concerned about Mum and her well-being and nothing else. We had little appreciation of how quickly the costs could mount up and we were subsequently presented with a huge contributory bill from the local council that ran into tens of thousands of pounds. This amount was paid to the council when we sold the house after Mum's passing.

It also felt like a blow that in spite of winning our case with the LGO against the council and Care Home 1, no real recompense was made against the suffering caused to Mum. It ultimately felt like those responsible received little more than a slap on the wrist. We never entered into the case with the intention of financial gain, but considering the failings detailed in the Final Decision we felt Mum should have been better compensated for the way she was treated. She had paid a great price for care she did not always receive. For all of her life, Mum worked hard and contributed towards the national budget via the taxation system. When the time came for her to require care, she had to fund this herself and received little benefit from all the years of paying Council Tax and National Insurance.

On the 7th of September 2021, the UK government announced a much-needed programme of reform to the adult social care system. Without doubt, the system needs to be reviewed and improved. It currently feels like the older population are increasingly being asked to pay into a system for which they often don't receive much benefit. Given that self-funders, like Mum, frequently pay more for their care, they are effectively propping up the adult social care system. Many argue that the intended reforms do not go far enough and, of course, there have already been delays and retractions by the government.

Then there is the emotional cost. Mum undoubtedly suffered unnecessarily, both at home with daily carers and while she was living at Care Home 1 and it was heart-breaking to see a vulnerable elderly lady treated in that way. We will forever be haunted by the sight of Mum hunched over in her wheelchair in the middle of the lounge at Care Home 1, her eyes full of pain and confusion. We felt angry for a very long time.

We always did our best for Mum but sometimes struggled to juggle family and work commitments with looking after her health and well-being, particularly in the early days of her diagnosis. This was accompanied by feelings of inadequacy and guilt. In fact, at times when we feel that Mum has suffered, the guilt has been overwhelming.

It has to be said that it frequently falls on family members to care for their loved ones, often with little support and at a huge personal cost to their own health and well-being. In addition to the intended reforms, there needs to be more help available to support those caring for relatives with dementia at home.

Dos and Don'ts

Do:

- Ask for clarification if you don't understand what your loved one is being asked to pay. If it's still not clear seek independent financial advice, or contact Citizen's Advice.

Facts and Figures

- The average cost of staying in a residential care home in England in 2019-20 was £681 per week, while including nursing care took the cost to an average of £979 a week (Care Homes For Older People UK Market Report, LaingBuisson, January 2021).
- During Dementia Action Week 2021, over 135,000 campaigners signed a petition, organised by the Alzheimer's Society (#CureTheCareSystem), calling on government to commit to publication of a clear, budgeted plan, and for reform to be underway that same year (Alzheimer's Society, September 2021).

Chapter 24
Reflections

The last years of Mum's life were a roller coaster of high and low points. And now that time has come to an end, we have been able to look back and reflect on all that took place. We always tried to do the best for Mum and her well-being and happiness was at the centre of every decision we made. Had we known at the beginning what the following years would bring, we would have done many things differently. We fought hard for Mum's rights but, in our opinion, the current system is flawed, difficult to navigate and full of pitfalls.

Throughout our time dealing with the UK adult social care system and the NHS, we met a diverse group of carers and medical professionals, most of whom were dedicated, kind and helpful, and we're grateful to all of them for their support over the years. Unfortunately, there were a few who did not meet the standards you would hope for in looking after the elderly and vulnerable individuals in their care, whether providing care at home or in a residential setting.

As has been documented, our first experience of residential care ended badly and Mum left there in poor health, from which we believe she never recovered. However, we are not alone in this experience. It was shocking and disappointing for us to find out that what happened to us is far from unique, as highlighted in the March 2023 report by Kings' College London led by Dr Caroline Green and backed by the Relatives and Residents Association (now Care Rights UK). The study found that nearly 6,000 residents in care homes were given notice to quit during a one-year period (January 2021–2022). At the heart of each one of these evictions is an elderly person whose needs should be the driving factor in any decision but, as our experiences have shown, this is often far from the case. It also appears that, what have been described as, 'revenge evictions' are sadly all too common. We were also disappointed to learn that 'notices to quit' were known to be a problem even before Mum went into residential care, so why was nothing done about it?

Our second experience of residential care was much more positive but coincided with a global pandemic. It left us feeling devastated that we weren't able to spend more time with Mum as she reached the end of her life. Lack of preparation and foresight by the government, coupled with lack of leadership and poor decisions, meant thousands of society's most vulnerable were separated from their loved ones just when they needed them most. Many, like our mum, would not live to be reunited with their families.

It also meant that care home managers and their

staff were operating behind closed doors with no one to routinely check on the quality of care being provided to residents. We would like to think that the vast majority of those care providers, around the UK, looked after those in their care to the best of their ability and tried, in some way, to breach the huge void in residents' lives created when family and loved ones were not allowed to visit. This was the case with Care Home 2, and we never doubted Mum was being well cared for.

We have subsequently learnt that Care Home 2 did not escape COVID-19, in spite of all the weeks and months of restrictions, and were saddened to hear that several residents, who we knew well and would often chat to when Mum lived at the home, had lost their lives. In a strange way, we are grateful this happened after we lost Mum, as we wouldn't have wanted her to end her life that way, or suffer the pain of losing people she had shared happier times with at the home.

We also feel angry and betrayed that while we were shut out of Mum's life, or struggling to communicate with her through a window, wearing a mask, certain politicians and government staff were 'partying' at Downing Street. A subsequent investigation and report by senior civil servant Sue Gray led to over 125 fines being issued for breaking lockdown rules, rules that had a devastating effect on those living in care homes and their families. In her report, Ms Gray accused senior politicians and officials of 'failures of leadership and judgement in No 10 and the Cabinet

Office'. To us, this proves how selfish and totally out of touch the people in charge really are. And these same people who showed a total lack of respect and disregard for the population they serve, are the ones responsible for making decisions about adult social care.

At the time of writing, in 2023, the situation in care homes remains serious, with staff shortages, long waiting lists and home closures adding to the pressure faced by the sector. We have been told this situation has been exacerbated by the effects of Brexit (the UK officially left the EU on 31st January, 2020), which has made it more difficult for EU carers, who provide such a vital role, to work in the UK.

Mum's fight may be over but the battle for reform, equality and transparency continues and we are proud to add our voices to all those campaigning for a better, fairer future for the elderly of this country. It is our hope that in future all elderly and vulnerable people will be treated with the dignity and understanding they deserve, however they are cared for and in whatever setting.

Acknowledgements

With special thanks to Zara and her amazing team at Care Home 2 who took in our Mum at an extremely difficult time and for taking care of her so well.

To the individual carers who showed kindness to Mum at Care Home 1.

You know who you are!

A special mention to Bob, Dot and their families.

Also to everyone who befriended Mum throughout her time in care.

Thanks to the many health professionals who helped us along the way.

Thank you to our beta readers, particularly Claire and Jane. Your helpful comments and feedback were invaluable.

Thanks to Trisha for her meticulous proofreading.

Useful Contacts

Age Concern
https://www.ageuk.org.uk

Age UK
https://www.ageuk.org.uk

Alzheimer's Society
https://www.alzheimers.org.uk

British Red Cross
https://www.redcross.org.uk/get-help/get-support-at-home

Carehome.co.uk
https://www.carehome.co.uk/advice

Care Rights UK
https://www.carerightsuk.org/our-campaigns

Carers Trust
https://carers.org

Carers UK
https://www.carersuk.org

Care Quality Commission (CQC)
https://www.cqc.org.uk

Citizens Advice
https://www.citizensadvice.org.uk

Dementia UK
https://www.dementiauk.org

Independence at Home
https://independenceathome.org.uk

Living Made Easy
https://livingmadeeasy.org.uk

Local Government and Social Care Ombudsman
https://www.lgo.org.uk

NHS (Equipment to make life easier)
https://www.nhs.uk/conditions/social-care-and-support-guide/care-services-equipment-and-care-homes/household-gadgets-and-equipment-to-make-life-easier

Our Dementia Choir
https://www.ourdementiachoir.com

POhWER
https://www.pohwer.net

Power of Attorney
https://www.gov.uk/power-of-attorney

Royal Voluntary Service
https://www.royalvoluntaryservice.org.uk

The Advocacy People
https://www.theadvocacypeople.org.uk

VoiceAbility
https://www.voiceability.org

World Health Organization (WHO)
https://www.who.int

Printed in Great Britain
by Amazon

28407991R00118